EMPIRE
ON
ICE

Willy Lou Warbelow

Other books by the author:

Head Winds
Kopotuk, the Eskimo
Child of the Equinox
The Guffinys' Chimney

EMPIRE
ON
ICE

by Willy Lou Warbelow

Main Street Alaska
Publishing Company
P.O. Box 252
Tok, Alaska 99780
1997

Dedication
"To my sister Hazel and brothers
Troy and Ralph, for their never
ending moral support.
And to Dr. Charles Keim whose
guidance and encouragement made
it possible for me to tell this story."

PT. BARROW

PT. HOPE

KOTZEBUE   KOBUK R.   SHUNGNAK R.   WALKER LAKE
                                      NORUTAK LAKE
        SHUNGNAK   KOBUK

                    ARCTIC CIRCLE
            HUGHES

NOME

                              FAIRBANKS
UNALAKLEET

                    CURRY

            ANCHORAGE

                    SEWARD

                    ALASKA

FOREWORD

To an 11-year-old Wisconsin farm boy in 1946, the thought of my newlywed aunt and uncle going off to a remote Eskimo village in Alaska to teach was very exciting!

Willy Lou and Marvin Warbelow moved to Shungnak, Alaska, 40 miles north of the Arctic Circle, to live and teach in an environment so completely different from the one we knew, that the comments from the family ranged all the way from "That's quite a challenge they face," to "They must be crazy."

As the years went by, Willy Lou wrote letters, long letters, describing the people and events that surrounded them on a day to day basis. My mother saved these letters in loose leaf binders. It was a family affair sitting around in the evening while Mom read these letters, so well written that they were worthy of re-reading several times. They later became the chronological journal that was the background for this book and others. The stories and events in *EMPIRE ON ICE* are not fantasy. They really happened to the Warbelow family, the last pioneers of our clan on the last frontier of our country, Alaska.

Peter M. Bodette

PREFACE

A REMINISCENCE

In the fall of 1945 I was on Guam impatiently waiting to be discharged from the Navy. I was dreaming of cars, dress clothes, and fresh vegetables. Even though the war was over, our mail still came late and in bunches. In one mail call I learned that my sister, Willy Lou, had married her college sweetheart, and they were on their way to a remote Eskimo village in the Arctic where she and Marvin would teach school. It was a lot for me to digest all at once.

I knew that Lou and Marvin were up to the challenge of the assignment. They were two people who thrived on challenges; and if they didn't get them naturally, they would make a few of their own. Lou had some idea of what cold and primitive Alaska would be like. We four Stellrechts, Hazel, Willy Lou, Troy, and I, were raised on a farm in northern Wisconsin where we once saw it -54 F; and thanks to the Depression, it was quite primitive. We had no electricity nor any of the modern conveniences that go with it. We did have a nice radio that our older sister Hazel had given to the family with her first few paychecks; but after the Depression struck, we couldn't afford batteries to run it. Dad always had a car, but if he couldn't get it started or if the roads were too bad, he would just hitch up a team of horses to a sleigh or wagon and get there that way.

But I had thought all that was behind us. Willy Lou had taken a teaching position in Madison just before the war so that I could attend the University there. We had become quite acclimated to modern conveniences, supermarkets, newspapers the same day they were printed, and an abundant social life. Fresh fruit and vegetables were always available to us. For anyone to give up all these things willingly, year after year, was hard for me to understand. In fact, it was unthinkable.

Needless to say, Lou and Marvin "made it." Our main communication over the next several years was by letter. Our four children and their four were in the same age group. Lou and I were very close as children and early adults, so I always regretted that our children lived so far apart. But thanks to letters, they grew up knowing one another as well or better than most cousins do.

Ralph B. Stellrecht

CONTENTS

11

CHAPTER I

TON'T FIGHT!

"Ton't fight! Ton't fight!" Even with the windows closed, the boy's frightened voice pierced the classroom walls.

Recess was almost over and I had just stepped through the door from my room to Marvin's to chat. We ran to a window to see what had caused the playground furor.

Two of my little first grade boys, John and Darrell, were in the midst of a fight; but what a strange fight! Their short, stocky shapes were exaggerated by the loose, bulky parkas and big fur ruffs covering the top halves of their little Eskimo bodies and the oversized mukluks that came halfway up their legs.

We watched John turn around and run away from Darrell as fast as his mound of clothing and the slippery snow underfoot would allow. In about 20 feet Darrell caught up with his classmate and gave John's shoulder a hearty whack with the flat of his hand. Then the process was reversed. Once his blow was accomplished, Darrell made an about face and began running in the opposite direction. Then John did likewise; and within another twenty steps, he caught up with his foe, slammed an open-handed wham on his back, and the entire process started all over again. Meanwhile, John's older brother Barry was running a continuous circle around the small battlefield, crying out over and over again, "Ton't fight! Ton't fight!"

For several minutes the fight went on, neither increasing nor decreasing in ferocity, and Barry never ceased running his circuit and pleading with them to stop.

"You know," Marvin commented, "Barry's big enough to pick one of them up in each hand and crack their heads together. That would sure stop this scrap in a hurry. But I wonder why he doesn't do it. I guess when an Eskimo fights an Eskimo, he doesn't do it white man style."

Recess bell ended the fracus, and I never asked my little boys what had caused their differences. But I recalled that in our few short weeks we had spent in this little Eskimo village of Shungnak, this was as close as I had come to seeing any sort of physical violence between two people. The children might squabble verbally, tattle, or even give one another an unfriendly little push in the hallway; but that was the extent of it. They weren't a violent or warlike race of people.

Yet they were not completely passive. Two days after our arrival, Daniel Stringer, a small wiry man in his early forties, made his first call.

He walked into the office without knocking, a custom in their own homes, but frowned on by most teachers. He was already through the office and at the kitchen door before we saw him. I was preparing lunch and Marvin washing his hands at the sink.

Hat in hand, and framed by the doorway between kitchen and office, he hesitated. "Good morning, Mr. Teacher! I'm Daniel Stringer."

Marvin's face immediately showed his displeasure at this intrusion. "I didn't hear you knock." He picked up the towel and began to wipe his hand. "What can I do for you?"

Daniel hadn't been prepared for such a curt reception. He flushed and his lips twitched a bit. "Well, I just come to say hello. Maybe we like to talk about some village business. I'm village chief. . . ."

The shrug of his shoulders that attempted to toss off lightly this last statement belied the flush of pride in his cheeks and the smile tugging at the corner of his mouth.

Marvin laid down the towel. "I'm Mr. Warbelow - Marvin Warbelow. This is my wife, Willy Lou. We call her Lou."

They walked together into the office, but not with the air of two new-found friends. Daniel had a definite feeling of rebuff. They settled into chairs in the office and the conversation resumed.

"Did you have some particular problem on your mind, Daniel?"

"Well, we always have plenty problem around village all time. These kits, they stay out late at night, they make plenty trouble. But now I think people wonder about you. You stop in village two day now and you don't come down to meet my people. When I'm chief, I always take new teacher down to meet people in village."

Marvin leaned back in his chair, his fingers laced behind his head.

"We'll come down to the village as soon as we can, Daniel; but right now it's more important for me to get this power plant working and some barrels filled with water, and the classrooms ready so we can start teaching.

"But I've already done a lot of thinking, Daniel. I guess I'm looking at some of your bigger problems. You know here sits a village of a hundred people and you don't even have a store of your own. You have to go ten miles upriver to get your groceries. That's all right for you fellows who have good dog teams. But I've been seeing old women starting out for Kobuk with a hand sled. I even saw one coming home carrying her groceries on her back.

"There's no post office either. There again you have to go all the way to Kobuk. Wouldn't you like it if we could start doing something about these things?"

"Yes, pretty good we have store old peoples all right. But you know trader at Kobuk been there many years.

15

He always been good to us. Store here in Shungnak make big trouble between us."

"You can't stop progress, Daniel. It's going to happen sooner or later anyway. You know that barge from Kotzebue goes right through this village every fall and on up to Kobuk with the very supplies that eventually you have to dog team back down to Shungnak. Wouldn't it be better if they stopped here in the first place? Hasn't it ever occurred to the people in the village here that you should no longer just be a satelite of Kobuk and stand on your own feet?"

Daniel smiled an amused little smile. "Sure, it sounds good, Mr. Warbelow. But just having our own store here won't give people more money to spend. My people are poor—very poor. It's money they need, too, and no way to get it."

"I've been thinking about that, too," Marvin assured him. "Lou and I come from farming country back in Wisconsin. I guess we just naturally look at the land and wonder how it can make a living for us. But you can't farm on land here in Shungnak where the permafrost is only six inches from the top of the ground. There has to be another way to make money, because even your furs don't bring you enough. I hear stories about this jade you have downriver. They say some outfit moved in last summer and has taken out a lot. Don't you think the Shungnak people should be trying to save that for themselves?"

"I don't bother much about jade myself. Maybe some other peoples do."

"I think it's worth looking into, Daniel. I'm already visualizing an independent village here—your own store, your own post office, and your own lapidary equipment where you can cut and polish your jade and make it into jewelry. There's your cash income right there! Just because you're a small village doesn't mean you can't prosper. The permafrost we're sitting on doesn't have to stop us. We can build right here on this spot our own little empire on ice."

"Okay, Mr. Teacher," the chief replied crisply, and stood up, beaver cap in hand. "Empire on Ice—sounds good,

16

but you're a cheechako. My people have been here long time. Maybe we know best way to live here in Arctic. I guess you ton't care about problems peoples have here right now."

From that moment on, I could see the beginning of a power struggle between my black-eyed husband and the black-eyed village chief.

* * *

I had a definite feeling of apprehension and wished Marvin had been a little less abrupt and a little more tactful. But how could I broach the subject without offending him? I'd been married to this man for a little more than a month, and I didn't really know him.

I waited for the door to close behind Daniel.

"You didn't do too well with him, did you?" I arched an eyebrow. "After all, he *is* the village chief."

"Look, Lou. We're here to do a job, aren't we? If we get snowed under by trivial things now, we'll never see the forest for the trees. I've had this store in mind since the minute we landed here. It should have been done years ago, but maybe they weren't ready for it. I think they are now. Daniel doesn't like it, simply because I suggested it first, but he'll come around. He'll give a little, and we'll give a little. It won't be easy, but that's the way it will be."

His words reassured me. After all, Marvin had already spent two years in the village of Elim down on the coast below Nome, and had some experience working with Eskimo people. And time proved him right about Daniel. The situation settled into an uneasy truce that managed to survive our three years we had to work together.

I mused in silence over the whole situation, and sighed. "Marvin, this all seems so new and strange to me—I'm in a different world. Did it really start just two short months ago, four thousand miles away on that platform at the railroad station?"

CHAPTER II

FROM MADISON TO SEWARD

I was at the station long before midnight, but already there were crowds of people milling around in the lobby and out on the platform, waiting for that train coming in to Madison from Milwaukee. Every train, every bus, and every plane during those memorable days in September of 1945 was loaded with boys coming home; and always there were crowds of happy, tearful families waiting to greet them. The long, horrible war that had dragged on for years had just a month before come to and end. Things were looking up.

Had there been a million men in uniform there that Sunday night, I could still have picked out his slim figure, the shiny black hair, and dark eyes. Marvin was home, and that evening I made the most important decision of my life. I chose the man I would marry.

"You'll never regret it, Lou," he promised. I never have.

I was just beginning my fifth year of teaching in the same elementary school in Madison, and just like that it came to an end. We packed our duffel bags, headed for northern Wisconsin where most of our relatives lived, stopped off just long enough to find a minister, and started for Alaska.

Confusion reigned in my mind the day we reached Seattle. Never before had I had a brush with a city of this size. Fortunately Marvin had run the whole gamut before, since he had spent two pre-war years teaching with the Bureau of Indian Affairs in Alaska and knew his way around. He liked to tell me about his first trip through Seattle.

"When I finally got myself to Seattle, I found out I had just missed a boat going north. I was mighty short on cash, so I had to set pins in a bowling alley for two weeks to make hamburger money until the next boat sailed."

By the time we had filled out reams of forms at the BIA office, completed our physicals, made a quick trip to Eddie Bauer's factory of goosedown clothing, and sold our car, I felt as though it had been the longest day in my life. I went to sleep with dreams about my red plaid all-wool shirt and white longjohns I had carried away from Eddie Bauer's with me that afternoon, all mixed up with horns blasting on Fourth Avenue and neon lights blinking in our hotel window. I even gave a little thought to the nice, rural woodsy farm I had grown up on in northern Wisconsin with wood stoves, an outdoor pump, and kerosene lamps.

* * *

Never before had I been so close to a ship, so the S. S. *Alaska* looked big and impressive to me. She was three decks high and carried about three hundred passengers. Our stateroom was on the main deck and about as big as an oversized closet. Double deck bunks covered the back wall. There was a small sink at one end and a chair against the other. This left about four square feet of floor space.

The dining room was beautiful. Maybe I was over-impressed with the abundance of food, since I had just emerged from four dreary years of meat and sugar rationing. Our first meal aboard was lunch. The entree of pork chops was followed by a parade of salads, relishes, vegetables, milk, apple pie, cheese, and cake.

"You'd better enjoy it while you can," Marvin warned me, "because this food is going to decrease in grandeur as we go north. You know once the fresh milk we had on board when we left Seattle is gone, there won't be any more."

"No fresh milk!" I went into a panic. "Why, even during the darkest days of the Great Depression, we always had all the fresh milk we wanted. I can't fathom being without it!"

Every inch of the five-day trip to Seward was beautiful. Our first day out we followed the Washington coast with Vancouver Island growing steadily in dimension. Then even Vancouver was left behind and disappeared an inch at a time in what I felt was the closing chapter of the first part of my life. As I look back now, my prediction was right.

By this time we were well into the fairyland Inside Passage. For two or three days we wound around through strings of islands, all heavily wooded with spruce and hemlock in the Petersburg area, Sitka spruce further north, and all this interspersed with yellow, red, and white cedar. The islands fringe the mainland Panhandle. Wherever we looked, there were endless strings of mountains alive with evergreens. The taller peaks were snow-covered, some hidden in the clouds. A flock of seagulls hovered constantly over the boat, waiting to dive for the precious cans of garbage that were thrown into the sea three times a day. They roosted all over the rigging, played around in the air between meals, and were born clowns. Their favorite passtime was to sit down in front of a big wave and ride over the top.

We spent hours on deck, leaning over the rail, trying to absorb in three or four short days a lifetime of beauty. This last part of October winter was fast moving into the north country. I was still wearing my little brown corde' hat I had worn the day I was married, a brown wool coat with no fur collar, and a cotton headscarf. These weren't enough. Soon I had to add my Eddie Bauer shirt to my cheechako clothes, but I still froze. Marvin was better off, as he had his mukluks and sealskin parka he had brought out of the Arctic after those two years of teaching at the little Eskimo village of Elim.

I hadn't been so relaxed in years. Back in Madison there had been the constant hassle of beating our way through traffic to and from school. Now, just six weeks later, that life was behind me. Before me, a door was opening into a world I had never dared dream about. I could close my mind on all those long, lonesome months without Marvin, because now he was beside me all the time, the sharp ocean wind blowing his black hair just enough to ruffle up the wave he so carefully pushed into place every morning. He was five feet, ten inches, lean and olive-skinned, never more than 145 pounds. Marvin was a moody person—never a middle-of-the-roader. His eyes were dark brown, but somehow you got the feeling they were the blackest black in the world. When he was at the bottom of the totem pole, his lips tightened, he was silent, and his whole person reflected his mood to the point that it reached out to everyone around him. But I like to remember those priceless moments when he was at the top of the pole. The black eyes sparkled, he was exuberant and witty, he laughed as though he had invented laughter himself, and his mood again radiated to everyone around him.

Leaning over the rail on moonlit evenings, we talked much about college days because we had spent our first two years of college together in Superior back in the mid-thirties. But then we lost contact. I went further south to teach and Marvin went north to Alaska. Nine years later when we met in summer school, the time seemed right. So here we were, baby-sitting the moon as each turn of the *Alaska's* propeller brought us closer to the little Eskimo village of Shungnak 35 miles above the Arctic Circle where we would teach for the next three years.

Our third day out we docked at Ketchikan, where I first set foot on Alaskan soil. Ketchikan, a town of 10,000 people, was shaped like a shoestring and squeezed into a flat beach about two blocks wide with the front row of buldings hanging out over the water on pilings, the last row crowded halfway up the mountain side. The town was alive with totem poles and full of whites, Negroes, Indians, and Chinese. Ice cream was seventy cents a quart and apples ninety-five cents a dozen.

After dark we pulled away from the dock with the whole mountainside alive with lights. Every light made a long, needlelike reflection in the water and multiplied the beauty of the whole town. I discovered, as we went north, that every coastal town almost duplicated the Ketchikan pattern—long, slim settlements hanging on the narrow ledge between mountain and ocean. I teetered between nostalgia for what lay behind and anticipation of what was ahead.

CHAPTER III

SEWARD TO KOBUK

Seward! You read about the town in geography books as though it were in another world, and here it was right before my eyes. The ship docked and we said goodbye to the little cubbyhole stateroom that had been our first home. With duffels on our shoulders, we followed the other passengers down the gangplank and up the path to the railroad station in this little rural-looking country town. Ketchikan and Juneau had been balmy and rainy, but Seward was something else. It was twenty below zero, and a wind that cut through us like a knife hit us in the face. By the time I had battled my way through the snow to the station, I was half frozen and out of breath. My cotton headscarf might better have stayed back in Wisconsin.

The train that came into Seward from Fairbanks and Anchorage once every two weeks had been waiting for us for hours. The Alaska Railroad is state owned and operated. It has no competitor, and the crew seemed to plan its schedule as they pleased. A good share of the passengers who started out in Seattle gradually left us as we stopped at ports along the way. But of those who

25

came as far as Seward, nearly all were taking the train inland. So the station was crowded with people checking baggage and buying tickets.

The train wasn't the fanciest in the world, but it got us there. We were in the heart of the mountains from the time we left Seward, and to be so close to the range we had watched from a distance that whole five days up the coast was a brand new thrill. At times we were so close to the spruce forests that the branches almost brushed the windows of our car. The railroad followed river valleys as much as possible, but at one point we made a complete loop, and from the top it looked like a big overgrown coil below us. Progress was slow because of heavy snows; and according to the stories we heard, the crew had to be prepared to stop at times and wait for moose to get off the tracks. The train was dusty, and in no time at all we were filthy. I made my first big blunder when I washed my beautiful red plaid shirt and yellow sweater in the washroom. I hadn't been warned of the hard water in various parts of Alaska, and my clothes came out three sizes smaller and feeling like boards.

We spent the night at the Curry Hotel. Curry was somewhere on the railroad between Anchorage and Healy, and the hotel was the only thing there. We were steered into a beautiful lobby and checked into our equally lovely rooms. Private baths weren't just run-of-the-mill in those days, but we had one. Dinner was elegant. When the evening meal was ready, someone pulled back a set of long, dark red velvet curtains that separated the lobby from the dining room. Each table had a white linen tablecloth and napkins. We had no choice of menu, but the food was good and the service flawless.

"Somehow, all this comfort and elegance seems out of place in a land of virgin forest and unpeopled country for endless miles," I sighed.

"Enjoy it while you can!" Marvin warned me. "It isn't always going to be this way."

Lunch the second day was another experience. The train stopped at the Healy railroad camp, and one of the crew members walked through our car to give us instructions.

26

"Everybody off for lunch. You can leave your belongings on your seats!" he sang out.

Obviously there was no restaurant of any kind in sight. We followed the crew into the railroad mess hall, and there was our lunch all laid out before us. Long, rough board tables with benches on either side filled the room. At the end of the first table were trays stacked with sandwiches and cake and mugs of coffee. We helped ourselves, and a lady collected our money. Then we lined up at the empty tables to eat. The railroad hands strayed in one at a time to look over the passengers and pass the time of day with the train's crew. No one seemed in any hurry to go.

When the crew had gathered all the local gossip to their satisfaction and put away several mugs of coffee apiece, they rounded us all up with, "Well, let's get back on the train and be on our way."

We were on the last lap of our journey that ended in Fairbanks that night.

* * *

Fairbanks was a city of six or seven thousand in those days, the first Alaskan town I had seen that was on level land and laid out square. It reminded me of towns I had seen in wild west movies. The buildings in general were small, sturdy, practical looking structures built to cope with some of the coldest winters on earth. The population leaned heavily toward the male sex. Most of the men who roamed the streets, drowsed in the chairs in hotel lobbies, or warmed the barstools, were hardy looking characters in beautiful Pendleton wool shirts, whipcord trousers, and fur caps. Many of them wore fur parkas and big mukluks.

"What do all these fellows do for a living?" I wanted to know.

"My guess," Marvin told me, "is that a good share of them are in from their mining claims for the winter and just killing time until they can get out to pay dirt again early in the spring."

We were fortunate to find ourselves a room in a wartime housing building recently converted to a hotel. The name of the hotel was "The Cheechako" which means "green-horn." It was, for me, at least, an appropriate place to take up residence.

"I feel as though I'm right back in Uncle Sam's barracks," Marvin declared as he dumped his duffel in the middle of the floor.

But the building was clean and comfortable and full of friendly people. Most of them were as new to the Territory as I was, and shared my excitement.

During those days at the Cheechako, Marvin's first order of business was to locate an air service that would take us to our village of Shungnak, about 300 air miles northwest of Fairbanks. When we stepped off the train that first night in town, we stepped into the bottom of a sea of the biggest snowflakes we had ever seen. A week later there had been no letup. Fairbanks was having a real snowstorm, and we saw it through to the bitter end. Marvin spent many sessions on the phone, pleading with every air service in town to make the flight. Of course he got the same answer from everyone—it wasn't flying weather.

We finally settled on one air taxi service that promised a flight the first clear day, so we made a trip to Weeks Field to work out the details. It developed that our pilot was an old acquaintance of Marvin's who had flown him once or twice up in the Nome country during Marvin's stay at Elim.

"What do you think our chances are of getting out tomorrow?" Marvin asked him.

"Your guess is as good as mine, but I'd say this storm has about worn itself out. We just might make it tomorrow. Yup—we just might make it." He peered out the window, pulled his lower lip in between his teeth, and nodded his head absently.

"What does the weather bureau say?" persisted Marvin.

"Well, I'd hate to stake my life on what *they* say!" He shoved his hands into his pockets, turned his back, and walked away.

The clerk at the desk was more encouraging. "You'll get out of here tomorrow morning," he promised.

I could see Marvin fast zooming to the top of the totem.

We bustled around and found a pair of real Eskimo-made mukluks for me. The soles were oogruk (hide of the big male seal), the tops calfskin trimmed with rabbit, and the ties of caribou—the most beautiful things I had ever seen, I thought.

Our pilot limited the baggage to four hundred pounds; so with this limit to comply with, we started repacking our duffels. We shopped for food supplies that turned out to be bulky and heavy, so we scanned our priority list religiously.

I can only guess at what kind of plane took us to Shungnak, because airplanes were as foreign to me then as freedom was to the serfs; but it was probably a six-place Norseman or something similar. There were four seats and a spacious baggage compartment that would normally have held another two seats. I bundled up in my wool clothing, mukluks, and choppers. They stuffed me into one of the back seats and packed luggage all around me. Then Marvin and our pilot climbed in, and we were off.

If the sun put in an appearance at all on that mid-November Sunday morning, it must have been when my back was turned. We had a solid gray overcast all the way from Fairbanks to Shungnak, a flight of about three hours. Halfway through our trip, we landed at the little Indian village of Hughes on the Koyukuk River. Hughes consisted mainly of a trading post owned and operated by a white couple, Mr. and Mrs. James. There were ten or twelve Indian huts scattered along the river bank, and that was it. The entire population was at the river to meet us. Our pilot had a conference with Mr. James about some gas he needed, and they headed out with a gas can and hand pump to some fifty-gallon oil drums lined up back of the store. Mrs. James insisted we come inside for a chance to stretch our legs and warm up. She didn't have to ask us twice, as we were stiff and cold; and we had hit some bad air pockets on the way, so my stomach was beginning to roll.

The floor plan of the James establishment was almost identical to every trader's store I ever saw in the next few years. Of necessity, arctic homes must be kept as

29

small as possible because of the heating problem. So the Jameses had built themselves a small one-room store with a two-room living quarters attached. Since the quarters were primarily for eating and sleeping, the store with its big oil-drum wood stove became the living room not only for the James family but for the native families as well. I seldom saw a trader's store without a circle of Indian or Eskimo villagers clustered around the stove, warming their fingers. This likewise was my introduction to true Alaskan bush hospitality in the form of a coffee pot. We had coffee and home-made spice cake while Mrs. James and I discussed our mutual love of cats, and I scuffled with the seven felines she had playing around her house and climbing through the rafters.

A half-dozen round-faced youngsters had followed us into the store and were grouped together in a little huddle near the door, watching us with their big dark eyes.

"What do you do about a school here?" I asked Mrs. James.

"Oh, we don't have one. But I hold school every day right here in the store, and they all come."

"You mean that you're a teacher?"

"No, no. Not at all. But we've borrowed books here and there, and I manage to teach them all to read and do their numbers. It's been this way for years."

The little group at the door grinned, happy to have been the topic of conversation for a few minutes, and suddenly with little whispers and giggles, they pushed and shoved at one another and tumbled out the door.

The farther north we flew, the more desolate the country became. By the time we left Hughes, the country was so covered with marshes, lakes, and rivers that there seemed to be more water and swamp than dry land. We flew over endless ranges of mountains, confusing to me because I had no idea of the lay of the land at that time.

Shungnak is located on the Kobuk River about two hundred miles up from Kotzebue. Three miles or so above Shungnak was a small CAA station, operated by a white couple, and a short airstrip built on a slope with the lower end running into the tundra. Seven miles further on was the little village of Kobuk. Our pilot turned around and alerted me as we flew over Shungnak. That spot didn't look like much of a place to set two people down and leave them. In fact, the village seemed to be only a small black smudge out in the middle of three hundred miles of wasteland. Growing darkness didn't enhance the picture.

Dick Collins at the CAA station told our pilot the ice at Shungnak wasn't safe to land on and the CAA strip wasn't any better, so he sent us on to Kobuk. We started letting down almost as soon as we left the CAA area; so by the time we flew over Kobuk, that settlement looked much more livable than Shungnak had. At least we could see the little gray cabins, each with its stovepipe oozing up a thin line of smoke.

Our pilot made a couple of circles to check out a safe landing spot on the snow-covered river ice in front of the village and to determine wind direction. Chimney smoke makes the best wind sock in the world; and years later I ran many times to turn up the thermostat when I heard Marvin coming in for a landing in our own planes, so he would have a puff of smoke rolling out the chimney to guide him.

"Looks as though the mail plane might have been in from Kotzebue," I heard the pilot shout to Marvin. "There's one set of fresh tracks down there." He tilted the right wing down so Marvin could confirm his conclusion, but I made no attempt to get close enough to a window to see anything. I didn't think I would know what an airplane track looked like anyway.

The skiis touched gently and we coasted like an overgrown toboggan until we slowed to a stop. The river bank was by this time lined with short, furry-looking humans; and before the prop had come to a complete stop, our audience had zoomed down the bank and we were completely surrounded. I had my first encounter with that thing I had read about in geography books since I was a little girl and dreamed about when I grew older—a real, live Eskimo.

31

CHAPTER IV

ESKIMO COUNTRY

Our pilot climbed out. "I brought you some teachers," he announced, then went around to the opposite side of the plane to open the door for Marvin. With the front seats cleared, he began plowing through sleeping bags, motor covers, gas cans, and our duffels in the plane. Eventually he found me and gave a hand so I could straighten my cramped, cold legs and tumble out the door.

In my first quick glance around at the circle of faces, I got a mixed-up impression of a rainbow of brightly colored calico parkas with round, black-eyed brown faces staring at us from inside their furry ruffs. Before we had time to wonder what we should do next, a fine-looking man stepped forward, and extended his hand to Marvin.

"I'm Charles Sheldon. You're the new teachers. The people here at Kobuk want me to say you're welcome. We're always glad when new teachers come."

All this in perfect English with an intriguing native twang to it! We found out as time went on that Charlie was the official spokesman when white visitors came to the Kobuk-Shungnak country, and very few of the older natives were capable of or willing to try speaking our language. They had long since developed the habit of letting Charlie do it.

With the flight to Fairbanks ahead of him and the daylight already fading, our pilot wasn't interested in any lengthy visits. All he wanted was to get on his way. So our conversation was cut short while everyone gave a hand at moving our luggage on to the river bank. There we gathered in a little group and watched as the prop started spinning, the motor revved, and with a few bounces of the tail to break the skiis loose, our plane went speeding to a takeoff and rapidly disappeared into the dusk.

I could feel the eyes of everyone on us, and little soft undertones of "Ah-h" and some exchanges in Eskimo among them; but no one other than Charlie spoke to us directly. Words weren't necessary. Their smiles and nods made us feel welcome.

Charlie pointed toward a frame building just a few rods down the river bank from us. "That's the store."

When you visited a new village, I had been told you went either to the home of the teacher, the missionary, or the trader. And since there was neither a teacher nor a missionary in Kobuk, we went directly to the store. Ray Chaplain's trading post at Kobuk was pracatically a carbon copy of the James store at Hughes. But there was one difference. Ray didn't come down to the plane to meet us as Mr. James had. Ray was even then an old-timer in the Arctic with forty winters to his credit. (Forty summers, too, I expect, but it's always the long, dark, cold winters we like to boast about.)

Ray Chaplain, the trader, was crowding sixty—a big, good-looking man and straight as a teen-age whippersnapper. I'm sure he had seen many pilots and many teachers come and go in his years on the bank of the Kobuk, and he wasn't about to go overboard in a gushy sort of way just because another pair of cheechako teachers had landed on his doorstep.

He was a perfect host, once you were under his roof.

Several of the villagers, including Charlie, followed us into the store. Charlie, who had seemed aggressive and sure of himself on the river, was no longer on home ground. Out-numbered by three white people, he remained silent; so Marvin became our spokesman.

"I'm Mr. Warbelow. This is my wife, Willy Lou. We're the new Shungnak teachers."

Ray shook hands with both of us, but didn't bother to introduce himself. Traders in the Arctic were well known and had the right to assume that everyone knew who they were.

We warmed our hands at the big oil-drum stove and exchanged courteous little nothings with him for a minute or so, during which time the store was fast filling up with the entire village population wanting to hear first-hand whatever we might have to say.

Ray's wife, Martha, a full-blooded aristocratic Eskimo lady with black-rimmed glasses and jet hair parted in the middle and pulled back into a pug, came out from her living quarters.

"Coffee on the table," she announced.

Ray began to warm up to us. "Come in and have something to eat," he invited, and led us into the next room.

So we sat down in Martha's kitchen to a mug of good, hot coffee and the biggest bowl of canned dark red cherries I had ever eaten, while Marvin and Ray discussed the foods available to us from the store shelves that we could take to Shungnak with us.

In spite of the warmth and food and the chattering, I was feeling a strong desire not to let Marvin out of my sight. He must have sensed this, because he waited until he had me involved in my dish of cherries before he disappeared into the store to start scouting for transportation for us and our gear to Shungnak.

The transportation he finally settled on was one Elmer Merina and his pathetic looking little team of five dogs. Marvin and Elmer loaded our food supplies and duffels into the sled.

Meanwhile Martha was scrutinizing my cloth coat and cotton head scarf.

"Too cold for you," she insisted. "Twenty five below zero already. That coat no good for you in this country." I began to protest. "Oh, I'm plenty warm. I've got snowpants on and my mukluks. I'm used to cold weather."

Martha didn't argue. She disappeared into the store and brought forth her own Eskimo parka in all its pink calico glory and insisted I wear it to Shungnak. I couldn't believe it, but then just about everything that was happening to me was unbelievable. The parka was the kind you put on over your head since there is no front opening. The colorful calico shell, with its wide ruffle around the bottom, was mainly for beauty. It covered a soft fur garment with the fur turned toward the inside. The cozy warmth of that mountain of fur I was buried in gave me a monstrous feeling of security.

The Kobuk was lovely. After all those hours of flying over what looked like barren wasteland, I was surprised to find our river lined with good-sized willows, and a little further back from the river on either side, masses of spruce and sprinklings of birch and aspen. The river was wide, and full of long, endless curves. Winds had blown the ice bare in some spots, but there was plenty of snow otherwise for us to follow the well-marked dog team trail that indicated heavy traffic between the two villages. Whenever a curve in the river turned too far in either direction, the trail made a portage through the woods and caught up with the river again where it curved back. The wind was sharp, so I pulled the big wolverine ruff up closer around my face and thought what a nice person Martha Chaplain was.

By the time we reached the CAA station, still more than three miles from the end of our trip, the dogs were exhausted, as were both the men who had walked the entire distance. Although Elmer had made space for me in the sled when we left Kobuk, I soon realized the dogs could never pull that load, so I too joined the walkers.

Mr. Collins, the CAA attendant, invited us in for coffee, but we declined. Marvin had a one-track mind at this point, and that track headed toward Shungnak.

"Lou, why don't you stay overnight with us and we

can take you on down to the village with our own team in the morning after Marvin has the building warmed up," Mrs. Collins suggested.

But I had no intention of letting Marvin get out of my sight, and no argument was enough to make me stay behind. So as soon as the dogs had rested for a few minutes, we started our last lap toward what was to be our home for the next three years. And how glad I was that I hadn't let the team go on without me that night!

CHAPTER V

AN ESKIMO WELCOME

That last three miles was torture for us. The men and dogs were as tired as I was. The parka gave me endless trouble. If I tried jogging, the hood slipped forward, and the ruff dipped down and blinded me. Then every time I stepped an inch too high, the toe of my mukluk caught on the ruffle on the bottom of the parka cover and I'd fall flat on my face in the snow. What a long three miles, I thought; but my pride wouldn't let me crawl back into the sled or even admit to Marvin that I was almost done in.

We were yet a half mile away from the village when Elmer let forth with one of the strangest "Yoo-oo-hoo's" I had ever heard. He called it loud and slow; and, in that silence that until now had been broken only by the crackling of snow under the feet of the dogs, it sounded like a giant yodel. In a matter of seconds, an identical call came from the village, followed by another and another until the calls were overlapping and mingling together in one continuous burst of sound. Added to this, a growing

39

chorus of dogs yelped their excitement. Elmer occasionally answered with another "Yoo-oo-hoo," and each time the response from the villagers and the dogs boomed louder and louder.

We had been on our last portage during this wild reception, and our trail came to an abrupt end when the trees suddenly gave way to the river again. Directly across the Kobuk from us, stretched out along the river bank and backed up into a steep hill, was the village of Shungnak. Even in the moonlight, we could see the outlines of fifteen or twenty cabins, some with smoke trails curling up from their chimneys, and a few that seemed dark and deserted. Our dogs picked up momentum when they realized the end of the journey was so near, and the dark forms of fur-covered people gathering on the opposite bank moved forward in one big mass to meet us. They surrounded us, everyone crowding in to get at least one hand somewhere on the sled to push, and the team was willing to turn the job over to them.

Out of the darkness from the forms milling around us came short, chopped-up questions:

"You our teacher?"

"You goin' teach us?"

"We start school tomorrow?"

"You come Kobuk in airplane? We see airplane go over."

The school was at the top of a hill behind the village, so up we started. The teachers who preceded us had left the village late in the summer, so there had been no school so far this year and no trail up the hill. There was three feet of snow, and the hill was steep. A dozen men helped push the sled and break trail. Marvin was right in the middle of it all, doing his share of pushing and exchanging all sorts of hilarious little quips and loud laughs about nothing in particular with his new-found companions. I tried to wade through the trail they broke and keep up with the gang, but soon I was bogged down.

From somewhere out of all this muddle, a big hand took mine and a man's voice said, "Here. I show you a better way." What a perfect way to meet one of the dearest friends we ever had—Robert Cleveland, being kind and thoughtful the first time I ever laid eyes on him, just as he was many times thereafter.

The dog trail and the foot trail up the hill took two different routes, but the dog trail was longer. So Robert steered me up the shorter one, holding my hand and half-dragging me, with a cluster of kids trailing behind us. I was hot and completely winded, but eventually the hill leveled off into nice, flat ground surrounding the government school and out-buildings. Marvin had the key and was already unlocking the school door with the aid of someone's flashlight.

He looked up as Robert and I emerged from the darkness into the small fringe of light at the end of the flashlight. "I lost you back down there at the foot of the hill, Lou. Figured I'd have to go back after you."

This must have been what the Eskimos considered a good joke, because a peal of laughter broke out from all directions. As it died down, Robert's voice sang out loud and clear, "You don't bother 'bout him. I take care him all right!" and the laughter rang again.

Marvin, Robert, and I groped our way into the dark entryway that led in one direction to the classrooms and in the other to the office and living quarters. Robert had one of those big-faced flashlights that was a coveted possession in every Eskimo family, and with good reason. With twenty hours of darkness a day and no electricity, an Eskimo village is the most logical place in the world for a flashlight.

"I school janitor," Robert paused inside the door just long enough to explain. "I find my way in the dark. You fellows just follow me."

He led us into the office and from there to the kitchen, just in time to make way for a thundering herd behind us. The whole crew that had followed us up the hill crowded into the entryway and the overflow filled the office. Someone must have given them a cue of some sort, because in unison they began to hoot and yell at the tops of their voices and began a rhythmic jumping

41

up and down with every foot hitting the floor at the same time, like a battalion of marching soldiers, until the whole building was jumping with them.

Robert ignored all this bedlam and went about the business of dragging a few sticks of wood out of a box near the kitchen range, laid them in the firebox with a bit of kindling that must have been right there waiting for us since the last teachers left, and in a matter of minutes had a fire going. He located an Aladdin lamp just like the one I bought my folks for Christmas the first year I taught school back in 1936, and in another minute we had both heat and light. Then, with no more ado he walked into the office and made a couple of hand signals to the cheering crowd. As if by magic the shouting and the jumping came to a halt; everyone yelled out a "good-night!" to us, and out the door they went.

What a relief! Marvin hadn't paid much attention to all this wild greeting, and I had pretended not to; but way inside me my stomach had been whirling like Mother's old butter churn, and I kept wondering what was going to come of it all.

"Robert," I asked anxiously, "what did all that mean?"

Robert laughed in delight. "Oh, you don't scare. They just make fun. Maybe you don't know Eskimo before."

I had to admit that I surely didn't know Eskimo before, and Robert chuckled to himself for some little time.

In the entryway that separated the office from our quarters was a door to the basement, and opposite it, another door leading to a small back porch. Even before our visitors had departed, Marvin was down the basement steps with a flashlight making a quick survey of all the goodies he had down there. Every male teacher in the Arctic had his own little heaven, and that was the basement full of light plants, out-board motors, tools, dried-up cans of left-over paint, cases of filters that never fit anything, and boxes of bolts and nuts that never fit anything either. In our case, Marvin's little heaven also included a big old jacketed coal furnace, a coal bin, and miles of pipe wandering around, crossing one another's paths, sometimes crossing their own, and eventually each one ending up at a hot water radiator in one of the rooms above. Robert, once his kitchen chores were completed, joined Marvin down under and spent a few minutes gloating with him over what Robert already knew was there; and then he, too, trudged down the hill.

The silence, the aloneness—it struck us both, but it was exciting.

"Do you realize, Lou, that we're standing here in the middle of a big, strange house we're going to call home and we don't even know what's beyond the kitchen door!"

It didn't take us long to find out. We couldn't carry the Aladdin around because of its fragile mantle, so we did our exploring at the point of a bobbing beam from the flashlight. Off the kitchen was a huge combination living-dining room, and beyond that were two bedrooms joined by a bathroom, tub and all.

"A bathroom, A real bathroom!" I cried. "And here you've been telling me we'd have to rough it!"

"Yes, but do you realize there's no waterworks to go with it? Robert tells me the water comes up the hill from the river and has to be stored in barrels."

So I shrugged that one off to be worried about later.

Back in the front entryway, we climbed an open stairway to a split-level upstairs that included various storerooms, and best of all, a nice, big home economics room equipped with an oil range, kitchen cupboards, and a half dozen long tables with benches.

My sister and brother-in-law had given us some blanket sheets for a wedding gift. Marvin had insisted that all four of them come north with us and I wondered at the time, what for? Now I knew. The bedroom end of the house hadn't had anything to do for the past three months except to get cold. And the kitchen range putting forth with all its heart and soul couldn't penetrate that far. We dumped a couple of duffels on the kitchen floor, located the ice cold blanket sheets, and warmed them in front of the oven door. Then, still in parkas and mukluks, we faced that icebox called the master bedroom and made up the bed. There were plenty of blankets at the station; and they, like the bedroom, had been getting colder by the month. We went to bed wearing as many clothes as we could, and shivered all night. To complicate the situation, Marvin was feeling utterly miserable.

"My chest is sure hurting," he admitted. "You know I ran most of the way from Kobuk and breathed in that icy air all the way. I don't think it did me any good. I've got pains all through my chest and back.

"I saw a hot water bottle in the dispensary. I'll put some of that melted snow we heated into it and that ought to make you feel better." But even with the hot water bottle and a lot of moral support, he didn't begin to feel better until morning. I had visions of his ending up with pneumonia three hundred miles from a doctor.

"You'd better not die up here," I warned him. "I'd stay just long enough for the funeral, but no longer,"

Toward morning we had the bed warmed up, but by this time the fire in the kitchen range had gone out. It was a losing battle!

CHAPTER VI

FIRST WEEK AT SHUNGNAK

Things are better when there's heat in the house, so that was our first order of business. Marvin brought the kitchen range to life again the next morning. We thawed out, melted some snow to wash our faces and boil a pot of coffee, and found some pilot bread and peanut butter to go with it. That was breakfast. This was the first I had ever heard the name pilot bread; but those big, round, hard white crackers were one of the mainstays of the Arctic. Their name became a household word with us, just as it did with everyone else in the north.

"Getting this furnace going will be a major project," Marvin predicted. "We can't fire up the furnace until we have water to put in the pipes, and the water is at the bottom of the hill."

"But didn't Dick Collins tell you there's some sort of a motor to bring the water up the hill?"

Beginning at the top of the hill beside the school, and ending at the river bank below was a narrow gauge iron rail track that carried a four-wheeled home-made flatbed.

This creation was let down to the river on the rails by cable where it was loaded with four 50-gallon oil drums filled with water, and then pulled back by means of a hoist powered by an engine. Our problem that Monday morning was that, in order to get the hoist motor started, we had to have hot water in it. So up the hill came buckets of water, carried by hand and heated on the kitchen range.

Robert had reported for work dressed in his canvas-covered parka and long white furry mukluks, with his reindeer-skin mitts hanging from a thin rope of braided wool yarn around his shoulders. He went at the water hauling like a trooper; and while the water was heating, he filled the kitchen woodbox for me.

Between armloads of wood or pails of water he tarried to strike up a conversation. I'm sure he had already sensed that Marvin was safely out of the way this morning, engrossed in the mechanics of his hoist motor.

One trip, just for openers, Robert commented, "You have many things outside we never see?"

I assured him that we indeed did, and promptly spun out a long list of things just to emphasize my point. "And then, of course," I said, "we have cow."

He made a pretense of never having heard of such a thing, and listened intently while I went through the whole story of what a cow was and what we used them for. I'm sure he had heard a similar story from every teacher who had passed through Shungmak for many years back.

"You teacher sure smart," he sighed. "You know every much."

"Not every much, Robert. You have some things up here I didn't know about. In my land when the summer days are long, the sun comes up in the east. It goes across the top of the sky and sets in the west. In Alaska, no. Up here, they tell me, it rolls around the edge of the world just above the ground all day long. It starts in the north, and finally comes back to the north where it disappears for a half hour or so around midnight and then comes right up again. I'm anxious for spring to come so I can see it. I never see anything like that before."

Robert was all wonderment. "You never see before?"

"I never see before!"

With an expression of extreme satisfaction that suggested a sudden new respect for his sun here at Shungnak, Robert pulled on his mitts and went out for another load of wood.

Nowhere had I ever learned much about cooking. So on that first Monday in my big kitchen on a gray November morning, I had to admit that I had never baked a batch of bread in my life. Marvin wasn't nearly as perturbed about it as I was. He insisted he had baked a few batches himself in his bachelor days at Elim and could give me some good advice. Besides, he had brought with him his mother's old cookbook that had in it, if you please, a recipe for making potato water yeast. Mr. Fleischmann hadn't yet come forth with his magic little packages of dry pellets, and the yeast foam I found in the cupboards had long since turned up its toes. Yeast foam was little squares of what looked like dry sponge and, when live, could be soaked in water for a few minutes to form active yeast. I tried soaking a cake or two, and when I got no results at all, resorted to the potato water. I peeled a few of our precious potatoes we had brought from Fairbanks, boiled them to a mush, and set them on the back of the stove to ferment.

By the time my potato mash could be officially called yeast two or three days later, I was hardly fit to be calling myself a cook. Marvin and I were both dirty, our hair was filled with coal soot, we hadn't had our fingernails cleaned for days, and we were wearing the same grimy clohes we had worn when we came. Marvin had donned a pair of blue and white striped coveralls with hammers and screwdrivers bulging from the back pockets. But he gallantly stood by the whole time I was mixing my sponge to give a little professional advice on how much flour to use, and to keep pushing my underwear and shirt sleeves out of the dough.

"I really ought to make up my mind whether I want to be a lumberjack or a housekeeper," I apologized, "but up here I guess I'll have to be a little of both."

Those first loaves of bread were all a bride could hope

for; and as the week wore on, I came forth with a cake, a batch of cookies, and a pot of good baked beans right out of my wood-stove oven.

We weren't really hurting for food except for meat, but we weren't having much luck with that. Joe Cummings, whose father Elo was the reindeer herder, promised to get us a piece of fresh reindeer, but we waited a long time for it. The herd was fifteen miles or so from the village, out on the tundra. At this distance, loose dogs were less apt to get to them, and it gave them a wider grazing range. But the herders sometimes spent several days at a time in the village without going out to check on the deer. By the time we got our meat, it was a welcome sight.

We had given ourselves one week to open the school, get the power plant and furnace in operation, and settle into our living quarters before we started classes. We could easily have found enough to keep us busy for two weeks, but we had feelings of guilt for taking even one. We found it difficult to explain to the villagers why school hadn't opened the morning after we arrived.

Chief Daniel came up the hill Wednesday morning to remind us again that it was customary for new teachers to visit every home in the village, and that he would be escorting us.

Marvin was still in his same dirty coveralls, covered with grease from the power plant and soot from the furnace.

"I'm not forgetting that, Daniel, and I think by Friday we should be ready to go. I can't go down there to meet my neighbors looking like this, and I don't want to get cleaned up until I'm through with the dirty work. I think I've got the bugs all worked out of the power plant, but I still have a lot of leaks in my hot water pipes. It's getting colder and darker every day. This has to be done first."

So the next two days we spent getting our building in shape for school and for the worst of the winter. Our office-dispensary that divided the kitchen from the main entrance to the building had cupboards full of medicine— most of them strange to me.

"What are all these brown bottles of pills?" I asked.

"Sulfa. Every kind of sulfa you can imagine. And most of it outdated. That pharmacist's mate training I got in the Maritime is going to be put to good use." He began a systematic housecleaning of the medical cupboards; and I fear more bottles of outdated medicine went into the garbage than stayed on the shelves.

I took on the chore of getting the classrooms in shape. Our predecessors had left the place neat, clean, and orderly. But the months between their departure and our arrival had done a good job of covering everything with a layer of dust. We had two good-sized classrooms off the main entryway with a long hall that opened into both rooms. The partition between the classrooms was made of four-foot-wide pieces of wallboard; but the building had settled over the years and must have been resting its elbows on the top of the partition, because several sections of wallboard were badly bulged.

We were working in our rooms one day when I called through the wall to Marvin, "I think it would be nice if we had a door between our two rooms."

He was evidently standing within a foot of the section with the most damage, because the words were hardly out of my mouth before he put a fist into the bulgiest part of the bulge, and the wallboard collapsed on my classroom floor. For the next three years we had an open doorway between our two rooms and could pass the time of day whenever we wished.

Then there were the Destitution girls. Welfare checks and unemployment compensation were as yet nonexistent, so Uncle had a different way of caring for our needy. Upstairs in one of the little cubbyhole rooms were piles of food and household staples. They consisted mainly of sugar, flour, salt, soda, coffe and tea, canned milk, and brownsoap. The villagers who couldn't provide their own food were put on our "Destitution list." Once a month the head of the family trekked up to the school office and took home $25 worth of supplies from the Destitution room. Unless there was no one in the family capable of working, they paid off the debt in labor. All our recipients were either unmarried mothers or widows, so I had plenty of help getting our classrooms scrubbed, dusted, and put in order. Robert assumed the task of visiting the girls on the list to tell them they were needed at school, and the next day I had Nellie Peterson and Ella Zeeter standing at the office door before we had finished breakfast, waiting to go to work.

We heard the outside hallway door open and the girls shuffling around making as much noise as possible to let us know they were there. I went out to greet them.

"We come to work in schoolroom for you fellows," Ella stated. "Robert tell us we should come up."

"That's right. We need you today."

The girls were both dressed in the universal calico parka cover with a fur reindeer parka underneath. Their hoods were pushed back off their round, olive-colored faces, forming soft warm collars to protect the backs of their heads and their necks. Both had jet black hair, parted in the middle, and pulled back into long pigtails, with sprinklings of loose reindeer hair scattered throughout.

I dragged mops, scrub pails, bars of brown soap, rags, and disinfectant out of a storeroom off the entryway and explained in detail what I expected them to do. Little did I realize that these Eskimo girls knew far more about scrub brushes than I did. They giggled, exchanged sparkly glances, and in unison said "Yis" to everything I said. Then they immediately disregarded every word and did the job as they saw fit.

But the morning ended in disaster. I checked on the girls occasionally and had no intention of dismissing them until I had given a final okay to their work. However, I discovered just before lunchtime that the girls were gone and all their equipment was stacked in the middle of the entryway. Marvin came in just as I was hauling the mop pail into the storage closet.

"What are you doing?" he demanded.

I could see a thundercloud forming. "Putting away the girls' cleaning things," I admitted meekly.

"What are *you* putting them away for? Why didn't they do it themselves? And anyway, how did they get finished so soon? Did you check up on them? Did they do everything they were supposed to do?"

I don't take criticism gracefully, and I was irritated. "Marvin, I don't know whether they finished everything or not. I haven't had time to get into the classrooms and look things over all that carefully yet; and besides, they left without my knowing it, so how could I tell them to put all this stuff back in the closet?"

"You shouldn't have to tell them. They certainly knew this wasn't where it belonged, and they knew where it should have gone."

"What makes you think they knew where it belongs? I'm sure they'd have been willing to put it back if they'd understood, but I don't think they did."

"That's it! They don't understand!" Marvin pounced on that one. "That's what's wrong with half the teachers who come to the Arctic. they make excuses for these people—they say they don't understand. Well, let me tell you—they *do* understand, and they'd have more respect for us if we treated them like the adults that they are. From now on, anyone who does a job for us is going to do it right. This is the last time I want anything like this to happen!" We both stormed out, but in opposite directions.

The atmosphere was cool the rest of the day. This was our first argument, and was about as close as we ever again came to one. Within a matter of hours, we realized that if we wanted to talk, we had to talk to each other. There wasn't anyone else to go to. We agreed that if newlyweds want a shortcut to learning to be compatible, the best place to do it is in an isolated village in the Arctic.

By Thursday night we had things fairly well under control, so Marvin sent word down to Chief Daniel via Robert that we would be ready to make our calls in the village Friday morning. Shortly afterward, a slim little girl in a puffy pink parka, beautifully decorated with braid, appeared at the door. Her white calfskin mukluks were crowned in wide brown strips of beaver and tied with strings of stained reindeer leather. She handed Marvin a note, written on a scrap of tablet paper and folded in

51

half. The note was addressed to "Teacher" and contained this message: "I am headacke. Tomorrow I am in bed. Respectfully, Dan. Stringer."

So Daniel set the day after all. We went on Saturday to visit the village.

CHAPTER VII

WE VISIT THE VILLAGE

During our first two hours in the village on Saturday morning, I learned more about Eskimos than any school book had ever taught me. I couldn't help but be a little amused as the thought flashed through my mind that so far we had spent more time being pupils than being teachers.

Daniel made the most of the situation. Promptly at eight o'clock he opened the door to the office and walked in. But at that point he half turned, facing the door he had just come through, gave a playful little tap to the casing as though he were knocking, and called out good naturedly, "Anybody home?" If anything could be called, "we'll each give a little," this was it.

In his gray sik-sik parka belted in a black and white calfskin fancy, and his knee-high summer caribou leg mukluks, with a jaunty beaver cap perched above it all, he looked every inch a chief. This was his day, and he knew it.

We slipped and skidded down the hill while Daniel coached us as to what we might expect to see.

"Some of our womens very poor. Lots of old peoples have hard time. Pretty hard for mans to take care two families. ANS should give some more help."

Well, I thought, at least I know what he's talking about now. I had already learned that ANS meant Alaska Native Service, the Alaskan branch of the Bureau of Indian Affairs.

The houses fitted essentially into one pattern. Each was built with a gently sloped gable roof and a tin stovepipe near the ridge pole. Windows were set low, the bottom edges not more than two feet above the ground. A typical house was equipped with a closed-in storm shed that served two purposes. It was a place to store wood and also took the brunt of the blast of cold air that ballooned in everytime a door was opened. The door leading from the storm shed to the main cabin was small and we had to stoop to get through it. Daniel, always in the lead, didn't knock, but walked in unannounced. This, I soon discovered, was the order of the day in Eskimo homes.

The house was lighted in most cases with a kerosene lamp or lantern or even a sputtering candle. However, the words kerosene belonged only in a cheechako's vocabulary. The proper term in the Eskimo world was coal oil. The average cabin was probably sixteen by twenty feet in dimension. The largest were not more than 24 feet long. This seemed ridiculously small to me until I watched the thermometer tumble to a chilly minus 50 degrees one day and decided it might not be a bad idea to heat a small house instead of a big one. My neighbors had already figured that out.

The standard stove was made of a 50-gallon drum lying on its side and supported by four short legs, with a door built into one end. The cabin walls were lined with home-made bunks, and some homes sported double-size Sears, Roebuck beds. Bedding seemed minimal and was often in a tangled pile on the middle of the bed. Caribou or reindeer skins, tucked under the beds, were no doubt brought out at night and used as bedding. Because the cabin was the only heated building a family had, it had to double as a workshop. Several of the men were building dog sleds; and since an average sled was from 12 to 16 feet long, it took up most of the floor space. The overhead cross beams held the walls in position and supported the gable roof. These beams were perfect storage areas for all sorts of belongings, mainly clothing.

The stage had obviously been set for our visit well in advance. The family was at home in every cabin—seated on the bed, on the floor, or on spruce stumps that made suitable chairs. Everyone, right down to the tiniest toddler, greeted us with grins and handshakes. We soon learned from Daniel's manner of introduction that the village was well supplied with babies whose mothers were the unmarried daughters in the family.

I didn't realize until we were back in the privacy of our own house what a social blunder I had made on that first visit to the village. But mine was a typical cheechako reaction. Every time we walked into a home, there was a period of what seemed an eternity of silence. No one said anything. I interpreted this as an awkward situation that no one but I had the finesse to cope with, so I began to enter each house with an overdone "Hello" or "How are you?" My greeting was always followed by the same stony silence until Daniel saw fit to start introductions.

Back home, I couldn't wait to make my comments about the situation. "They surely don't know much about greeting people, do they? If I hadn't broken the ice in some of those homes, we'd probably still be standing in one of them waiting for something to happen!"

Marvin arched an eyebrow. "I'm afraid you were quite out of order, young lady. Eskimos can chatter and laugh a mile a minute once they're warmed up to the occasion, but they're never in any hurry to get started. Next time you go into one of their homes, it will be best just to outwait them."

The smallest and poorest home in the village was a little shed-roof structure not more than eight by twelve feet in dimension. One lone window had most of its panes broken and stuffed with weather-gray rags. The door was low, and even the front side of the cabin was barely high enough for us to stand upright. The back side was a wall not more than three feet high. There had originally been a floor made of handsawed boards, but most of them were broken or had disappeared, with the bare ground showing in between the few that remained. But the two sisters and their children who lived there were some of the most sparkling and happiest people in the village.

"Did you girls build your own cabin?" I ventured.

"Oh, no!" explained the younger of the sisters. "Papa build it lo-o-ng time ago! We always live here our whole life!"

I was sure she felt the same love for her little log shed that I felt for the big home my father had built and raised us in back in Wisconsin.

"Those women need bigger cabin all right," Daniel commented as we walked on down the path, and then he was silent. He seemed to have no solution to the problem.

One cabin stands out in my memory, and that was the only real sod home in the village. It was legitimately called an igloo and might have been one of the reasons for the stories we've heard about Eskimos who live in snow houses. The igloo was built around a rectangular hole dug about two feet deep into the ground. The upper part, shaped like half an oil drum cut lengthwise, was built completely of pieces of sod cut from the tundra. These sturdy chunks made a wall a foot or more thick, with the dirt, held together by masses of roots, forming the inside walls, and the tundra grass covering the outside. The only window in this picturesque little shelter was in the center of the curved roof. The hole was covered with a pane made of seal gut, impossible to see through; but it let in light and held out wind, rain, and cold. The gut had been split lengthwise, cleaned and dried, and then laid in overlapping strips like shingles to form a perfect window. Since the house was nearly half underground, the door was even shorter than those in other cabins. We had to bend to get through it, and walk down two steps to the floor. An igloo was the easiest type of cabin to heat and amazingly homelike once you were inside. Its biggest drawback was the fact that every spring the family had to move into a tent for a few weeks, open up the door of the igloo, and let it dry out.

Like many of the older people we met that day, the ancient woman who lived here could neither speak nor understand English. Daniel went through his introductions in Eskimo. She grinned, nodded at us, and spoke a few words.

"She say it's good we have teachers," Daniel told us.

"And you tell her we think she has a good house," Marvin returned.

Daniel repeated the words to her in Eskimo. Her face broke into another big, toothless smile, and with a soft "Ah-h-h" and a nod of her head, she let us know we had been accepted.

Daniel, always the perfect showman and never to be underestimated, saved his own home for our last visit. The house was spotless, well built, and well equipped. His wife, Dora, was busy twisting caribou sinew into thread for her skin sewing; and his three pretty daughters were knitting away in proper silence on woolen gloves decorated with elaborate patterns in bright colored yarn. Daniel introduced his women folks in his most austere voice, but with little trickles of pride oozing through in spite of his attempts to hide them. None of the women lifted her face enough to look directly at us, and they spoke as little as possible.

Marvin made an attempt at conversation. He lifted a strand of Dora's sinew and slid it along his hand. "Are you going to use this for mukluks?"

She gave her husband a quick glance, and seemed to sense that he expected her to answer. "Maybe," she said quietly, and went furiously on with her twisting.

I thought I might have better luck at making conversation. Addressing the three girls generally, I asked, "Do you make up your own patterns for all those mittens?"

With faces still lowered, and never missing a stitch, the three daughter exchanged glances. Daniel's face was expectant, silently commanding one of them to speak.

Finally the youngest who had delivered the note to us

two days before, said softly, "Yis," and the women's share of the conversation came to an end.

Although Daniel was trying to be matter-of-fact about the affluence of his home, he couldn't resist showing us his dining table—a luxury denied to most of the cabins. About the size of a card table with eight-inch legs, the table could be set on the floor during meals as the family sat cross-legged around it, then leaned up against the wall to be out of the way. Daniel didn't make any verbal issue of the fact that the Stringer women were the best skin sewers in the village, but we noted several pairs of beautiful mukluks and beaded slippers lying on display in prominent places. Nor did he mention the fact that his daughters were beautiful and that the oldest one had the longest hair in the village. He didn't need to mention it. The facts were obvious.

Daniel, in a jovial mood, walked halfway back through the village with us before we parted ways. We knew that he expected some sort of comment from us.

Marvin offered his hand for a farewell shake. "Thanks for showing us the village, Daniel. You have some fine people here. I think we're going to enjoy them."

Daniel flushed with pleasure. "Well, I try to do what best for my people. Sometimes pretty hard, but I do. Any time something you want, just come ask me."

He meant exactly that. This was his way of telling us any move anyone made in the village must first have his blessing.

We started home in silence, each deep in his own thoughts. Meeting the people in their own homes had opened up another new world for me. I was bursting with enthusiasm to get the show on the road. The promise that started us to Alaska in the first place was still there: to make a contribution in the teaching profession.

Marvin, with his greater experiences in the villages, could discern essentially what I could see, but also knew we faced other tasks that we wouldn't settle in the classroom.

"The essential goals of teaching will eventually pay off," he assured me. "They'll help us to accomplish things that need to be done in the village. I'm more convinced than ever now that Shungnak must eventually stand on its own feet. We've got to get a store established here, and a post office. But there's not enough income here to give people a decent living. Right now I can see only one possibility—develop the jade."

We would accomplish these tasks in the next three years, and in doing so we'd learn as much from our students as they would learn from us.

But for now, as we were nearing the end of our first real trip through the village, each of us once again was lost in our whimsical thoughts.

CHAPTER VIII

SCHOOL OPENS

Those first few days at school I'll never forget. We had about 35 school-age children in the village to begin with. But word got around that school was opened, and every few days another family came mushing into the village with its belongings piled high on the sled. The next morning we'd have some strange, black-eyed bashful youngsters padding in big mukluks into the classrooms. Our students could be generally divided into two groups—those whose families lived permanently in the village so the children could go to school regularly and those who were still nomadic. The youngsters in this second group posed a problem. Their schooling was a hit-and-miss thing. They were usually in school for such short periods of time that it was impossible for them to pass from one grade to the next. So it wasn't uncommon for a child to be ten or twelve years old and still in the first grade. I had the first three grades, and Marvin the fourth, fifth, and sixth. A student seldom went further in school than that, and our biggest class was always the first grade.

I often wondered, back in my teaching days in Wisconsin, how one coped with a non-English-speaking child, but now I found out. The bilinguals were priceless. I was forever calling for help from one of the older students to straighten out a state of confusion that existed between one of my first graders and me.

One morning I said to a little fellow who had just taken off his parka, "It's cold out this morning."

He turned around and started to scoot back into his parka.

"Stop him!" I called to an older boy who had just come in the door.

They spoke a few words, and the bewildered little fellow finally put his parka back on the hook.

"What's the matter with him?" I asked.

The older youngster giggled. "He think you tell him to go home!"

Getting in and out of those parkas (The Eskimo always called then "parkys") was a sight to behold. A parka was loose and shapeless and made with neck big enough to slip easily over its owner's head. Each child had his own hook in the hallway where he could hang his parka and mitts. He'd walk up to the hook, bend his head over, and catch the edge of his hood on the hook. Then he would raise his hands over his head and back off until he had uncocooned himself, and the parka was hanging in place. After school he reversed the process—pulled the bottom of the parka over his head, eased up toward the top until his head raised the hood off the hook, and put his arms into the sleeves. Then he gave himself a few violent side-to-side shakes while the parka fell into place. The girls' parkas were long—only six or eight inches from the floor—so it took a few more shakes for them than it did the boys, whose garments ended above the knees.

All this was hard on hairdos. Every head had a smattering of reindeer hair from the lining of the parka among its own dark hair, and anyone who didn't carry a comb and take the time to smooth his hair down usually went through the day looking a little ruffled.

I remembered earlier experiences with teaching first graders and my mad dashes to the Hektograph machine every day after school to prepare stacks of seat work to keep them busy the next day. So I was in a state of panic when I faced up to a roomful of first graders that first day of school.

"How will I ever be able to keep up with enough seatwork for all these kids? I've never had so many first graders in my life!"

"Don't worry about it," was Marvin's response. "They don't work that fast. I had classes nearly that big at Elim and I had all six grades. It won't be any problem."

"But you probably weren't as conscientious about it as I am. Maybe you didn't expect them to learn as much as I will."

Both his eyebrows went up and he gave me a long, hard look. "They learned."

Marvin was right. Language barriers slowed my classes to the point where we sometimes spent several days on one piece of seatwork.

We soon found out that our attendance records would never win any first prizes. Circumstances at home, usually something beyond a child's control, kept many of them out of school a good share of the time. Hardly a day passed that some youngster didn't come with a note from someone explaining why so-and-so wasn't going to make it that day. This is a smattering of the little torn scraps of paper and tiny note pad sheets I still keep packed away in a cardboard box:

Dear varbelow

well Im not gonig to school today cause my mother gonig to see snares and Im gonig to stay with my little borther. I would like to come to school Everyday. But me little borther nobody to stay with that why I will gonig to stay home.

Agnes

63

Techer
David is stomach ache also bowls move. he didnt go to school this morning.

Your friend
Daisy, W

Say Dolly is out of school this after noon. she the only one who could work in house Bessie is went after fishing camp.

Henry

To Mr warbelow
Im not gonig to school again. I like to go to school But Im head ache that why Im not gonig to school

Agnes

The last hour of every day was crafts class time. Robert, the school janitor, taught the boys the art of snowshoe and sled making in the shop. Mrs. Ticket, one of the oldest women in the village, trudged up the hill every day in her plump pink parka with her wolverine ruff pushed back like a high collar, framing her white hair. She carried under her arm her day's supply of birch bark that she had peeled from trees along the river bank, and spruce root pulled up and stored in her cache during the summer months. Because permafrost comes within a few inches of the surface of the ground in the Kobuk country, tree roots tend to go not too deep, but to parallel the ground. They are easy to dig out. Mrs. Ticket, whose Eskimo name was Ayarlook, had a fascinating tatoo down the middle of her chin—one straight line about a quarter of an inch wide—that had been made by rubbing coal ashes into the skin, I was told. If that was actually how it got there, I wasn't sure, because I heard varying stories as to why it had been done in the first place. According to one story, it denoted marriage. But I have also heard that it indicated membership in one of the high-class families in a village. Whatever it meant, Ayarlook Ticket was one of only three women in the villages of Shungnak and Kobuk who could boast of a tatoo mark down her chin. Ayarlook was the

Our first year at Shungnak.

School and living quarters in Shungnak.

Marvin with hoist car that carried freight and water up the hill from the river.

Upper grade children.

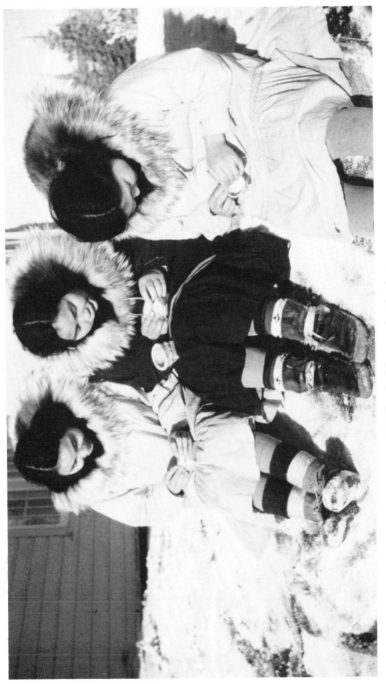

School girls weaving baskets.

School girls on a frosty day.

Tommy and Clara Lee and children.

Kopotuk, smiling on a bright sunny day.

Dog team ready for a trip.

Dog team heading for a load of wood.

Marvin explores a neighbor's cache.

School students.

Willy Lou and otter skins in front of school.

Filling water barrels to go up hill on the hoist.

George Cleveland and a nice catch of fox pelts.

Aged Eskimo women while resting on the ice.

Going for a pail of water.

best basket maker in the village, and every afternoon she sat on a small chair in the classroom to teach the girls the secrets of basket making. She coached, scolded, and praised as the need arose, and reprimanded in the strictest fashion those girls who used her hard-gained bark and root promiscuously, yet consistently turned out inferior basketry. Every month we would cull the poorest baskets, miniature sleds, and snowshoes, and mail the rest to our arts and crafts headquarters in Juneau to sell. I remember one little girl who used more bark than any other child in the class and never made a saleable basket in three years. But there were others who always turned out beautiful work. Daniel Stringer's two youngest daughters, Betty and Hope, were among them.

CHAPTER IX

MAKING OF THE PARKA

Marvin still had the sealskin parka he wore at Elim. Now I wanted him to have one made for me, but he refused.

"You're the one who needs a parka, and this will be an ideal time for you to visit the homes and do your own dickering."

So I had either to do it myself or freeze to death, and I had nothing but trouble. Irene Douglas, a cute little widow who lived in the first cabin at the foot of the hill, was the official parka maker in the village, but I got off on the wrong foot with her.

"Irene, I need a parky and everyone tells me you're the best parky maker in the village."

"What kind parky you want?"

"I really don't know what I want. What kind of skins do you have?"

"I got no skins. Maybe you have to get some other womans. You like caribou? I think some caribou skins in village."

"Okay if you say so." I was encouraged to be making progress. "I'll get some caribou skins. I'd like some fur around the bottom and one of these pretty belts you call fancies. Will you make it for me?"

She grinned, gave her shoulders a little shrug, and said, "Maybe."

After all this discussion, and then I get an answer like that! I hadn't yet learned that "maybe" means "yes," so I left, a bit miffed at her flippancy.

Sarah Cummings who lived next door to Irene was a real horse trader. She not only would make my parka, but she would sell me some caribou calfskins, although she either couldn't or wouldn't tan them and she couldn't make the fancy. (The fancy is the strip of deocrative black and white calfskin just above the wolverine strip that forms the bottom edge.) I didn't know where all these skins she talked about were coming from until she started dragging from under the bed—not only caribou, but beaver, muskrat, and marten, and strips of wolf and wolverine. Sarah was talkative and I got my first real lesson in identifying fur that day. But she drove a hard bargain, and the skins didn't look too good to me, so I decided to play it cool. She didn't make the sale.

Serena Bond was easier to deal with. She was a widow who supported two small children and her old mother, Mama Corning. Everyone was busy when I stopped in. Mama, in her bright blue calico parka cover, with a crown of beautiful white hair pulled into a pug at the back of her head and several loose strands floating about her leathery face, was on the floor scraping skins to be tanned. Serena was hammering caribou bones into pieces and grinding them into pulp by hand with a mortar and pestle made of wood.

"When I get it all smashed and boil it, the bone and marrow come apart from the lard. When I put it through a strainer, I have nice lard and I can give bone part to my dogs."

"You mean you can get enough lard out of this stuff to bother with?" It seemed hard to believe.

Without getting off her knees, Serena reached into a

box sitting on it side against the wall, and lifted out a two-quart tin can filled with spotless white lard she had already rendered, and I mentally chalked up one for the Eskimos.

A young relative was making Serena's house his head-quarters that winter since his family lived down river. Like a lot of other fellows, he was making a 16-foot dog sled right in the middle of the cabin floor. The sled was in the assembly stage, and he was binding the parts to-gether with narrow strips of tanned sealskin he had brought from the coast near Kotzebue. The inland Eskimos, some-times called the caribou Eskimos, made annual trips to the coast with their raw furs to barter for sea products from the salt water Eskimos. Families who had enough fur to bring back a poke of seal oil were the envy of the village. A poke was a beheaded sealskin scraped clean of fur, with the ends of the legs tied shut, and the open neck area filled with fresh oil and tied. "Just like Wesson oil," someone once told us.

But back to my parka. Serena had what looked like three nice caribou calfskins she would sell for ten dollars. I was skeptical because of their size.

"Irene told me to look for caribou, but she didn't say caribou calf. Wouldn't grown caribou skins be better?"

Serena translated my question to her mother. Mama elicited a soft low "E-e-e. Ahnee," and shook her head. They both laughed, and even the young man who was pretending to ignore the fact that I was there looked up from his carpentry long enough to grin.

"You no want big caribou skin," Serena told me. "No good for parky. Hair too stiff. We never make that kind much." She shuddered at the very thought of it.

So with my calfskin bundled under my arm, I set out again.

Mrs. Ticket, mother of Irene Douglas, was sitting cross-legged on the floor in front of her stove, peeling young willow sticks and splitting them in half lengthwise to use for baskets and nut cups in her crafts class. I showed her my skins and asked if she would tan them. But she couln't speak English. So when our sign language finally

85

proved too limited for such a technical transaction, I called in a stray youngster who was wandering past the window to interpret.

Mrs. Ticket sat listening politely as I explained my problem to the little fellow. Then I listened just as politely as he relayed my inquiry. She was thoughtful for a moment. Then with a few Eskimo words, she raised and lowered various fingers to clarify to him the financial part of the arrangement.

The child turned to me. "She say yes she can do it. She want one dollar fifty cents for one skin if she tan it."

The deal was finally closed, and I unloaded my skins on the floor.

Clara Cleveland lived in the opposite end of the village, and I queried at every cabin between Mrs. Ticket's place and hers before I finally found someone who was willing to make my fancy.

Clara was preparing the evening meal while her husband, Tommy, and two children sat by watching her.

"Clara, I'm having a parky made and I need a fancy for it. Many people tell me you can make one. How about it?"

Clara became suddenly flustered, "I ton't know. Maybe I can't do too good."

"Oh, sure, you can. I *know* you can do it better than I can!"

This was an Eskimo-type joke and the family laughed. Clara finally looked at Tommy for an answer to my request, and although they could both speak English, they carried on their discussion in Eskimo. Then Tommy became the spokesman.

"She say she can make, but she need calfskin."

"I can get calfskin from Harry's store at Kobuk," I told him. "Then if I furnish the calfskin, how much will she charge me?"

More discussion in their native tongue. Then Tommy again addressed me: "She ton't know how much she charge. She say tomorrow she can see Irene and ask her."

I'd made a complete round of the village, and went back up the hill feeling quite satisfied with my shopping tour.

"How'd you make out?" Marvin asked me, and leaned back in his swivel chair at the desk.

"Marvin, did you know that you don't make caribou parkys out of big caribou skins? Yo make them out of small ones. They're softer, and they look nicer. And would you recognize a marten skin if you saw one? It looks so much like a mink that you really have to know your furs to tell the difference. It's even sort of hard to tell the difference between a beaver skin and land otter too if they take the guard hairs off. Guard hairs are those long hairs all mixed up with the short ones. They're coarser and tougher than the short underhair and they protect it from rain and stuff. And they don't make fancies from native tanned skins at all. You have to buy Holstein calfskins tanned Outside, but Ray's store—"

"Wait a minute! Wait a minute!" Marvin teased. "Did you come up here to be a teacher or a scholar?"

"I'm going to be both, and so are you! And you know it!"

The next morning, Rose Bond, Serena's daughter, handed me a note when she came to school. The beautiful little message said, "who's going to tanning. My Mother can tanning if you want to. Your friend, Serena Bond."

I chalked up another one for Serena and Mama Corning and wished I could have accommodated them. But Mrs. Ticket was already at work on my skins, and I knew she would do a good job.

The ruff proved to be another hassle. I didn't have much trouble locating a super-nice strip of wolf and delivered it to Sarah, my seamstress; but there I ran into trouble. With the fur in hand she gave me an unbelieving look as though she couldn't decide whether I was being defiant or just stupid.

"Woman ruff ne-e-ever make from wolf!" she exclaimed. "They always make from wolverine. Only mans have wolf."

I knew that, but wolverine ruffs were made by layering

several strips of fur like shingles; and the ruff stood up too straight and formed what I thought would be a wall for wind to hit from behind and blow the ruff down into my face. I explained this, but Sarah had no intention of breaking tradition. So I settled for the wolverine ruff and never liked it. Fortunately my parka hung togther only a year and then began to shed so badly I had to have a new one made. I went through the same hassle with Irene a year later; but she gave in, and I spent the next fifteen years wearing a man's ruff on a woman's parka.

CHAPTER X

CHRISTMAS HOLIDAYS

Christmas season is the highlight of the year in a native village. We had our school program on Christmas Eve, and the church had one Christmas night. There were no individual family Christmases, so it was a community affair. We had a big tree at school and another one in the church.

Marvin and I were meticulous decorators, so with the help of the whole school, we spent hours making decorations and dressing up our tree. I finished it off with a long accordian-pleated strip of heavy aluminum colored paper to cover the base, never thinking about what would happen when people started piling packages on top of it.

The afternoon before our program, we had the school open so everyone could bring his present, and I stayed in the classroom to help with the labeling. Most of the older people couldn't write. By late afternoon, that tree was piled up past the first circle of branches. No one wrapped gifts—just tied tags to them. They exchanged skins of all sorts, mukluks, fancies, and socks and gloves they had bought in Kobuk. One fellow even gave another a string with nothing on it but a note that said, "One sheafish to be delivered after Christmas."

The whole village turned out for the program that night, even the old wrinkled bent-over ancients who probably hadn't been outside since Christmas the year before. Charlie Douglas, one of our older schoolboys, was Santa Claus, Marvin had him well-padded with pillows, never realizing what would happen to them before he made his final exit. Charlie was elated over his role and bounced onto the stage on tiptoe in the manner of a ballet dancer. The schoolchildren up front began to sing softly a rhythmic Christmas song. Charlie rose to the occasion and did a jaunty few steps in time to the music. The kids, encouraged by his cooperation, raised their voices a bit, increased the tempo, and began to clap their hands in time to their chant. Charlie's feet rose higher and hit the floor harder with each step. A few of the older people began to clap and hum, first softly, then louder; and Charlie had to increase the size of the floor space he was using for his dance. Now he was bounding from one side of the stage to the other. His feet alone could no longer express the story he was trying to tell, so his hands began to take part in this fabulous exhibition.

In a matter of minutes the whole room was booming with song, hand clapping, foot stomping, and cat whistles all mixed together. Charlie's feet were spending more time in the air than on the floor. He jumped as high as he could at every beat, threw his body and hands and head around in unbelievable contortions, while he zoomed back and forth. The pillows began to shift from his chest to his belt, then slipped below his belt to his abdomen, and finally one of them sailed completely out of his shirt and landed on the stage beside him. He paid no heed—just kept cavorting, landing with one foot and then the other on the pillow that had once been his stomach, and didn't seem to notice it at all. His cap and mask bounced with every bound, went further and further askew, and finally they both tumbled off and went sailing into the audience.

Charlie was wild-eyed, his face purple, and beads of perspiration from his forehead were rolling in rivulets down his cheeks. He was puffing air through his mouth; and finally, exhausted, he danced off the stage, half undressed by this time, and collapsed onto the floor behind the curtain. Had he been in any shape for a curtain call, it would have been justified. The stomping and clapping and cheering went on and on. Then we gathered up Santa Claus's scattered costume, put him back together again, and the program went on.

The Junior Red Cross had sent us boxes of gifts for the school children, and there were sacks of candy and fruit for every person in the village. We were thankful no one had been short-changed, because Marvin and I were surrounded by gifts we hadn't expected. I received a hand-carved ivory bracelet from the lay-reader missionary's son, a purse made of two wolf heads and lined with bright red crepe from Mrs. Chaplain at Kobuk, a sik-sik skin, birch bark basket for berry-picking, hand-knit gloves from one of the Stringer girls, wolf-head mittens, and a yellow ribbon. Marvin was given a piece of jadeite from Jade Mountain down river, an ivory letter opener from the boy who made my bracelet, and a black bearskin rug.

The gift presentations were accompanied by jesting and laughter. So when the bearskin was pulled from the tree branches and handed to Martin, the crowd cheered and clapped.

Marvin pulled his eyebrows together and pretended bewilderment.

"What do I do with it?" he asked, addressing his question to the whole room.

"Use it like sled!" someone shouted. "Sit on it and slide down hill!"

Laughter again, but the skin did make a wonderful sled to go scooting on down to the village. When it needed cleaning, I simply turned it upside down with the fur against the snow, and did my sliding that way.

I had arranged for Jennie Stringer to make me a beautiful pair of beaded calfskin slippers with hard oogruk bottoms for Marvin's Christmas present, and had them hanging on the school tree for everyone to admire. Unfortunately, he put them on and wore them for the rest of the evening. As soon as the schoolroom cleared out, he started into the basement to check the light plant. But he got there sooner than he expected. Those slippery oogruk bottoms hit the top step and that was all. In one nonstop hurdle that would have rivaled Santa Claus's capers that evening, he cleared ten steps and landed on the basement floor.

* * *

So much for the white man's Christmas. The school was our domain. We imposed our customs on the children and they went along with it gracefully. But the Friends' Church down in the village was in their world. So Christmas night they did it their way and it was our turn to conform,

The Collins family mushed their dogs down from the CAA station Christmas day to eat reindeer steak dinner with us and go to the church program. We were still sitting at the table involved in lengthy discussions of our various childhood backgrounds and reminiscing on Christmases long gone when Dick suddenly looked at his watch and exclaimed, "Do you realize that program is starting right now!"

We bounced off our chairs and began scrambling for parkas and mitts.

"Do you suppose they'll start it without us?" we girls wondered.

But there was no need to worry. The church was packed and everyone was waiting for us. A front-row bench had been reserved, and three ushers escorted us. Chief Daniel was master of ceremonies.

"Welcome, Mr. and Mrs. Warbelow, and Mr. and Mrs. Collins," he greeted us. "Come right up here and sit down. The boys have some seats for you."

Chief led the prayer, announced each number as it was presented, and passed out gifts with the help of three or four young fellows he called from the congregation. Everyone, from children to old people, took part in the program. The children did almost all their numbers in English and then in Eskimo. The oldsters, with a maximum of delay and confusion in each case, went to the stage in groups to sing. The delay didn't bother the audience. No one was in a hurry to bring the evening's festivities to a close.

At one point, Daniel dangled three strings from the ceiling and tied a muffin to the end of each at face level. The corners of his mouth twitched despite his attempts to look severe. "You, Jim, come up here!"

A teen-age boy scrambled to the stage.

"And you, Frank—George—come on up!" Daniel indicated each boy with a jerk of his head and two more lads jumped on stage beside Jim, eyes twinkling with excitement.

Daniel tied each boy's hands behind his back with a big handkerchief. Then with a child positioned behind each muffin, he gave the command "Go!" and the contestants raced to see who could eat his muffin first.

The older people had evidently never learned to sit on benches for any length of time, because they had a space on the floor for them to sit up front, close to the stage. I recalled one night earlier at a school meeting when the oldsters started getting tired, they slid from their benches to the floor and slept.

Their tree decorating customs were quite different from ours. The tree had been too tall for the room. But while we would have trimmed it from the bottom, they cut it off at the top. The blunt top that remained pressed tightly against the ceiling, forming a soft green ring against the logs. It was decorated with rolls of crepe paper, carefully rolled and saved from previous Christmases. I felt a sharp pang of homesickness when I recalled how we did the same thing in the litle country school I grew up in back in Wisconsin.

Just as our tree up at school had been the night before, the tree at church was stacked with gifts; and the branches were loaded with small things such as gloves, socks, and miniature dolls. Each gift had a lengthy card attached. The ushers distributed gifts one at a time, and each waited his turn so the notes on the cards could be read aloud.

Most of this was in Eskimo, each note being followed by laughter and much hilarity. If the note was a special prize, the usher would read it a second time in English so we four whites could have a chance to laugh, too.

* * *

Christmas night at church was only the beginning of their gift exchanging. The next night they went back again. This time people had a chance to give gifts to those who had given to them the evening before. So it went for several nights, each gathering having a smaller turnout, until they gave up and announced it officially ended. Gifts that were received Christmas night often showed up on the tree the next night as a gift to a third person, and that person in turn could pass it on if he wished. One of the men confided to Marvin that he started out giving a package of cigarettes and ended up with a nice pair of leather gloves.

While the gift giving was gradually wearing itself out those evenings between Christmas and New Years, we spent the days having games and races on the river ice. There were dog races and snowshoe races, but the ball games were the wildest of all. Every afternoon the whole village congregated on the river for a game they called football. Their ball was made of reindeer hide stuffed with reindeer hair and shaped like an oversized baseball. If there were any rules, we never figured them out. The game started with someone's kicking the ball, and from then until the end it was every man for himself. They rolled, tumbled, and jumped on top of one another in one big monkey pile with the ball at the bottom. Whenever the ball slipped out from under it all and either rolled or was kicked clear of the tangled heap of bodies, the race started all over again. Everyday we had casualties, and Marvin had to bandage someone.

The basketball games were no better. Some teacher before us had unwittingly mounted baskets at each end of Marvin's classroom, and we just as unwittingly had failed to take them down. We had to clear all the furniture from his room—it doubled as a gym. Their basketball didn't have any more rules than the football did. They usually played men against the women. Once the referee tossed the ball for the two centers, he ducked his head, ran for his life, and wasn't heard from again. The game went on nonstop with no hold barred, until the teams were too tired and mutilated to go any further. Marvin got dragged into playing a game one night, and it cured him forever. He came out of that ordeal with fingernail gouges all over him and his new Pendelton shirt ripped to pieces.

But the ball games and races, like the revolving gift giving, finally died out. Little by little the village settled back to normal. It was a Christmas season we didn't forget.

CHAPTER XI

WE GOT NO GRUB

That first winter strung out endlessly. The sun had dropped lower and lower around the fringe of the horizon until by mid-November it disappeared completely. For two months the only proof we had that it was still in existance was a gloomy twilight effect that brightened briefly at noon. By early afternoon we had total darkness that lasted until mid-morning the next day.

The lowering sun was paralleled by a lowering of morale throughout the village. Wood was always in short supply, and fires often went out. Coal oil was expensive, so the families often sat around in the evening with no light other than that thrown off by the heating stove. One evening when I stopped in to visit an old lady who lived alone, I found her sitting cross-legged in the middle of her floor with her parka on and the ruff up around her face. She had neither light nor heat in the cabin. Ella Zeeter, one of our Destitution girls, came to the office one day after school. She was obviously upset about something.

"We got no soap," she stated abruptly. "Our hands all

97

chap from cold water and no soap. We can't make our hand clean. We can't make our dishes clean."

"Ella," said Marvin, "you get twenty five dollars destitution every month. You'll just have to figure things out a little better. If you need more soap, then let's cut out some of the sugar or the tea. There's no way I can give you more."

"We need sugar and tea, too. Twenty five dollar not much for Mama and me and brother. We need soap now and we need grub."

"What did you have for breakfast?" Marvin asked her.

"Only mush. That's all we got in house to eat. Just mush. Other teachers didn't make us wait so long."

"It isn't the end of the month yet, Ella, and I can't give you destitution ahead of time. It isn't mine to give. It belongs to the government. But I need slippers. If Mama want to make me some, I can pay you for that."

That took care of the situation temporarily, but it wasn't the real answer to a universal village problem. Marvin wasn't very sympathetic, though. He had spent two years on the coast where fish were plentiful and ducks, geese, and ptarmigan were everywhere. He recalled that every spring he would go on an egg hunt with one of the village families and rob the nests that were in abundance. As far as the people of Shungnak were concerned, he felt they were either lacking in ambition or were poor managers. It took a year of living there to find out for himself that there was no great abundance of either game or fish before he realized his error.

Ella wasn't the only one having problems. The chant of "We got no grub" became routine. Marvin was losing patience, so one day during an afternoon chat with several companions down in the village, he broached the subject of doing some muskrat trapping under the ice. Silence from all directions made him think no one knew what he was talking about. So he explained how you can build a box with one side open and set a rat trap in it, chop a hole in the ice to submerge your box, then wait for your victim. No one seemed to understand, so he gave up in frustration and came home.

"Lou," he announced, "we're going to show these Eskimos how to trap rats in the winter time. I'm fed up with this 'got no grub' stuff."

He built the box, and the next night after school we tramped a mile out across the tundra to a slough where we chopped our hole in the ice and set the box with the trap in it down into the mud. For three nights after that, as soon as the classroom doors were closed, we hiked out to check our trap. Marvin was getting discouraged.

"I know it will work," he insisted, "because I've seen it done. but I'll have to admit it's a darned hard way to make a living. Besides, I just about freeze to death on these trips out into the tundra. You'd think longjohns and whipcord trousers would keep my legs and seat warm, but they don't."

At this point, Robert came in the back door with an arm-load of snow-covered wood.

"Robert," Marvin asked him, "how do you manage to keep your legs warm these cold days?"

Robert's face broke into a smile, and with a twinkle in his eye, he dropped his wood into the box, then reached down inside the front of his trousers and pulled out a tanned white rabbit skin. "I just tuck this down inside pants between my legs every morning. Keep me warm all a time!"

So that night we rummaged through the arts and crafts materials in our storeroom to find a rabbit skin for Marvin.

Our fourth night on our trapline we finally lucked out. Marvin headed straight for the village. The usual gang of hanger-ons were standing around a crackling fire where one of the fellows was cooking dog food in half a big oil drum.

Marvin tossed his frozen rat on the ground. "See this, fellows! Didn't I tell you it's possible to trap rats under the ice?"

After a leisurely silence and some unconcerned glances at the little blob of fur on the ground, somene finally commented, "Ya—old timer do that some time too."

But that was the end of it. Not one man made any effort to set a rat trap under the ice.

Marvin and I gave it some serious thought. The listlessness of the children trying to do their lessons made us realize they weren't being properly fed. The high percentage of tardiness indicated that didn't have the energy or the desire to get up in the morning to go to school.

"We've got a lot of problems here," Marvin decided. "These people will go hungry before they'll break tradition. They don't hunt rats through the ice even though the old timers did it. There's got to be a reason why. Maybe rats aren't as plentiful as they were years ago and they've established the habit of limiting their trapping season to let the rat population build up."

"Whatever the problem is," I added, "it's reflecting on our whole operation here at school. There doesn't seem to be any way to get these kids to school on time. I don't really blame them. If I had to get up in a cold room and start out without breakfast, I wouldn't be much interested either. You can tell which kids come from homes with good providers. Those families are up and have fires built in the morning and a breakfast cooked, and the kids are here by nine o'clock. They turn out better work during the day, too."

Then came the answer to our problem. Shungnak was chosen as one of three villages in Alaska for experimental hot lunch programs that winter. The Alaska Native Service had inherited tons of army surplus foods to be used for the project. The food they had might not always be what we wanted, but at least it was a beginning.

"This will give us a chance to get on better working terms with Chief Daniel," Marvin said. "We'll give him every opportunity to take over the leadership here."

He invited Chief to the office to talk over the possibility of the hot lunches and found him enthusiastic. Chief called a meeting of the entire village to work out the details. Marvin explained the program to the village. Charlie Sheldon, who had mushed down from Kobuk for this important occasion, interpreted for those who couldn't understand English.

"We want to make this a breakfast instead of a lunch. We'll feed the kids right at nine o'clock so they'll be sure to get to school on time. They'll have full stomachs when they start their reading classes. If the destitution girls do the cooking, they can get breakfast too. Maybe we can invite the little kids that aren't in school yet to come up for breakfast and then stay in the classroom for a half hour or so to do some kindergarten work."

Charlie passed all this on to the roomful of parents, and they nodded assent and crooned soft approvals.

Then Chief Daniel took over the meeting. We were allowed a limited amount of supplies from the store at Kobuk to supplement the government issue, so several of the men who had the best dog teams were assigned the task of making the trip to Kobuk for food.

We would need wood for the stove to cook the hot lunches, so Chief Daniel decided that while half the men went to Kobuk, the others could cut wood. Enthusiasm was in abundance. When the teams arrived from Kobuk that night, we already had a prosperous looking pile of wood stacked up at the back door ready to be carried upstairs to the lunchroom.

Having the village share the responsibilities would make them feel more comfortable about accepting the idea of their children eating breakfast at school, we thought. But there were still those who hesitated. The native missionary's wife came to us one day just before we got things underway.

"We've never accepted charity," she explained. "We can make our own living. We don't need anyone to help us."

It took considerable explanation to convince her there was nothing dishonorable about her children's eating breakfast at school.

Our three or four destitution girls moved right into the role of cooks. They took turns every morning coming up at eight o'clock to start breakfast. Marvin always had the wood fire started for them and usually a big pot of water on heating. Breakfast included some strange menus. Not only did we serve oatmeal porridge, but baked beans, macaroni, spinach, and always our basic pilot bread, peanut butter, dried fruit or juice, and canned milk. Before long, I had our cooks trained in the art of making sour-

101

dough bread from dark flour, so the pilot bread became only an emergency thing used between batches of home made bread.

The children liked having a school breakfast. Once it was established, the tardiness ended. They were braver about crawling out of a bedroll and making a run for school when they knew there was a hot breakfast waiting at nine o'clock. It didn't take them long to learn that if they missed the nine o'clock bell, they likewise missed breakfast.

Our youngsters were extremely self-conscious about this strange new way of life. They sat primly lined up on benches with eyes on their food, and ate in silence. But their plates were always cleaned, and we could see an improvement in the caliber of their school work.

No one ever asked ahead of time what we were having to eat that morning, but there was always some chatter about it as we left the lunchroom and went downstairs for classes. For the primary and pre-school children, the new words they were learning in the English language were a challenge. The older children evidently managed to inform the younger ones during the meal what they were eating, because I would get such comments afterwards as, "We have bean for breakfast?" or "I—eat—soup?" Their big black eyes turned up as they spoke, always with a questioning look in them, sparkled when I nodded and agreed that they had really just had beans or soup.

Only once did we serve a breakfast that went almost one hundred percent into the garbage bag we saved for someone's dogs. We had an abundance of both white and yellow cornmeal and big cans of molasses in our store-room. To serve yellow cornmeal was useless. Yellow cornmeal was often used for dog food, and wasn't fit for human consumption, altough they ate the white meal without hestitation. So we decided one morning to have corn bread and molasses. Ella, the cook, was unhappy about it.

"We never eat anything like that," she said. "I ton't think kits will like it!"

"They never ate it before because they haven't had the

chance," I argued. "Lots of people eat corn bread and molasses and like it."

But Ella was right. The plates were hardly touched, and in spite of urging and coaxing from both Marvin and me, the kids settled for a breakfast of milk and fruit.

After school that day I went to the village to do some errands and stopped in at Violet Perry's house to see the new baby. While I was there, her little first grade boy came in, picked up a razor-sharp ulu (knife), and began shaving thin slices of meat off a hind leg of raw, frozen caribou lying on the table. As he cut them off, he popped each one into his mouth. I was astounded, but Violet completely ignored him.

Finally I asked, "Violet, won't he cut himself with that ulu?"

Violet shrugged. "No. He do all time." And the subject was closed.

Many times has the picture of that little fellow who had thrown away his cornbread and molasses and then gone home to eat raw caribou flashed through my mind.

When I related the incident to Marvin, he was amused. "Have you ever seen a white man eating raw oysters?" he asked. "Is there really any difference?"

CHAPTER XII

NOATAK HUNTERS

In February, five sledloads of people went up on the Noatak River about a hundred miles north to hunt for caribou and wolves. They went every winter and usually managed to get back the first week in April; but this year, for some reason, they didn't return. Then we had an unexpected warm spell, and the snow melted to the ground in some places. The tundra stretches for several miles back of the school to the foothills, so for days we had little groups of people at the top of the hill watching the tundra trail for signs of our hunters. The weather was so much colder on the other side of the mountains that we knew they would never realize what was happening in Shungnak.

Finally, a week behind schedule, our caravan appeared, but they had real difficulty making those last few miles with their loaded sleds. With more meat than they could carry, they had been double-tripping forty miles at a time. They'd cache their loads and then go back to get the second load.

It had been two months since the hunters left the village, and with their sun and windburn, some of them were hard to recognize. Jonas Bale got home without a mishap and then broke his sled runner in two going down the hill into the village. He spent the next day repairing it, and the following day, he retraced the last forty miles for his second load. They brought all the caribou they could haul, a dozen or so wolf pelts, and a nice brown bearskin.

I wanted that bearskin in the worst way. A beautiful thing, about seven feet long, its thick long hair rippled from one color into another, from light tan to dark brown.

"Jonas," I asked in an off-hand way, "what do you intend to do with that skin?"

In an equally off-hand way, he responded, "Well, if I can't sell it, I'll make leather out of it and use it for dog harness." An impressive silence reigned, while he rolled his tongue around behind his lower lip and scowled at the sun. "Daniel sold one about that size last year for fifteen dollars."

I didn't press him any further, but how I did want that skin!

"If you really want the bearskin," Marvin advised me that evening, "you'd better start dickering before he begins to strip it."

I think he wanted it as much as I did but was afraid the brown bear would turn out to be a white elephant.

It became a game of who could outwait whom, and Jonas played his end of it as well as I did mine. Every day I invented some reason to walk past his house, fearing each time that the bearskin spread out on the fish drying racks would have disappeared and gone the route of dog harness; but it never did. And Jonas, who didn't normally spend a lot of time visiting with us, wandered to the top of the hill nearly every day.

"When spring come, no good to stay in house," he explained. "A man need to get out in the sun."

So we passed the time of day and he'd tell us yarns about early days in Shungnak when history was being made, but we never touched on the subject of the bearskin.

106

Jonas was a character—a sort of smug, easy-going fellow always looking out for Jonas, who got a big laugh out of seeing anyone else get into trouble. He was amused to no end when a pilot from Fairbanks who had done considerable flying in the area for a few months left the country owing a big gas bill at the Kobuk store. He wasn't even perturbed when one of his best friends was arrested and taken to the jail in Nome. And he thought it mighty funny when a native woman from Kobuk refused to take some letters to Kotzebue for us when she flew out with Archie Ferguson. But it was even funnier to him when Archie didn't show up to get her. She sat there three weeks waiting for him, and he still hadn't come.

"Serves her right for not taking the teacher's mail!" Jonas declared.

One day Marvin had a big project going up at school. He had cranked up a new motor and used it to pull the old hoist motor up the basement steps so he could install the new one. Jonas was a cat skinner in his spare time and had worked as one for Arctic Exploration Company the previous summer in an asbestos mine up back of Kobuk. Motors he couldn't resist. When he heard the hoist motor banging away, he was at the top of the hill in short order.

So just like that, I said, "Jonas, I'll give you ten dollars for that bearskin."

He jumped at it so fast, I wondered if he would have taken five.

Jonas's wife Lillian was a sweet person. The bearskin transaction created a bond between our families, and I was happy for a chance to break the ice and feel free to stop in at the Bale home for visits.

I knew from looking over village records in the school files that one of her children had been born "on the trail to Noatak" during an annual spring hunting trip.

"Lillian," I asked her, "how do you manage with diapers when you're on the trail like that?"

She smiled in amusement at my stupidity. "It's simple," she said. "We always carry baby on back inside our parky.

107

We put tundra moss in bottom of back of parky first, then baby on top. That moss make diaper for many hour before we have to change again."

There's quite a bit to be said about—both for and against—this business of back-packing the baby. The hood on a woman's or girl's parka differed from that on men's garments. A little peak was built into the bottom half of it so when a baby rode in his mother's parka, his head fitted perfectly into this peak and his face snuggled against the back of his mother's head. If the child was old enough to stand up, getting him into the parka was a simple matter. Mama backed up to Baby, stooped down, holding the back hem of her parka out away from her legs so she could settle it over the child's head with both of them inside the parka. Then she'd hoist him up by the seat until he was in place at the back of her shoulders with his legs around her waist. She tied a long, decorative sash around her waist, creating a seat for her passenger, and they were ready to go. A baby that was too small to stand up had to use a different route to the passenger's seat. Mama put it up under her parka from the front, then wiggled and twisted and eased it around to her back. Little girls were expected to take care of the family baby a good share of the time, and it wasn't unusual to see a small girl toting around in her parka a baby sister or brother half her own size.

When the men were away from the village for days or weeks at a time on hunting trips, the women were doing the same thing on a smaller scale at home. Each had her own little trapline within walking distance of the village and would check it every day or so. We would see them, with babies snuggled inside their parkas, and snowshoes strapped to their feet, leaving the village early in the morning, and coming back just before dark at night.

Whether these months of riding piggyback during baby-hood had any effect on bone development or not, I couldn't say. But adult Eskimos' legs were definitely shorter and more bowed than those of most white adults.

CHAPTER XIII

THE ARCTIC BOYS

We heard about the Arctic boys for months before they became a reality. Once or twice a year several dog teams from the little village of Anaktuvuk, some one hundred thirty miles north, mushed down to the Kobuk country in sleds loaded with goods to barter. About half the men in the village made the trip to Shungnak and Kobuk, while the other half went further inland to Bettles.

For days from late March on, there was always someone and sometimes several people at a time, standing at the top of the hill near the school looking out across the tundra, each hoping to be the first to sight those little moving black dots emerging from the wooded foothills area into the flat, open country. The dots would be the dog teams, and the first person to spot them and shout out, "Arctic boys!" was the envy of the village.

When it finally happened, school was in session. We heard that first loud "Arctic boys!" and then it was followed by another and another, and the whole village seemed to erupt. Our two classrooms, always quiet and orderly, turned into complete bedlam. Like forty little bombshells, the kids bounced out of their seats, dived into the hallway, and without taking time to grab their parkas, poured out the front door.

Marvin had first made a firm, and finally a feeble attempt to bring order out of chaos; and in complete defeat and bewilderment we stood in our empty classrooms to collect our thoughts and wonder what had happened. But within seconds it occurred to us that we should have followed the kids, which we did, just in time to come nearly being run down by the whole village huffing and puffing from that trip up the hill. Everyone was shouting that same "Yoo-oo-hoo" we had heard on our arrival in Shungnak a few months earlier.

Once it was established that the dark line moving across the flat was indeed the Arctic boys, half a dozen men ran home, hitched up their teams, and started out full bore to greet the travelers. To host one of the visitors was an honor, so it literally became a race to see who could reach them first and have his pick of the guests he would invite to stay in his home. The visitors, in general, stayed with the families that had hosted them on previous trips, and the man of the house proudly referred to his guest as "my pardner."

The teams were a pathetic looking little group of animal-hood when they finally ended their long journey. The dogs were smaller than those in Shungnak, thin and badly treated in some cases; and at this point they were exhausted. The five or six drivers were small men, dressed completely in caribou fur or skins. Anaktuvuk was truly one of the most remote villages left in the Arctic. It had no school and no airfield, and of course no postal service. The only contact the village had with the rest of the world was this annual or semi-annual trip to the Kobuk country and Bettles.

Hilarity reigned that night. There was much feasting, and a continuous string of people moving from one house to another to swap yarns with each of the visitors. By the end of their second day, the men were rested and feasted enough to think about some recreation, so the native dances began. People collected every night in one of the larger homes. The drummer sat on the floor cross-legged and beat out his rhythmic booms while the villagers and their guests danced their hearts out. It took some time for them to warm up to the occasion, and at first only a dancer or two would get out on the floor for a few minutes and then quickly retire to spectator status again. But as the room grew warmer from the heat of many bodies crowded into it, blood flowed a little faster, hearts raced, perspiration stood out on foreheads, and the dancers gave way to complete abandon until the wee hours.

During the several days the Arctic boys were in Shungnak, they kept us busy in the office. Each one had an order to be made out to Sears, Roebuck and Co. for supplies for his own family or a neighbor's. So Marvin leafed through the Sears catalog making out orders for clothes, tools, and maybe even a toy or two. The orders wouldn't be picked up until their next trip to Shungnak several months or even a year later. But it usually took months for parcel post to get to us anyway, so they were apt to get their mail as soon as our own people did.

"Where will you get money to pay for these orders?" Marvin queried one of the men.

"Oh, we get from Ray Chaplain when we take skins to Kobuk."

"And what if your wife doesn't like what you picked out?"

Our guest laughed. "Oh, she like, all right!"

Legal papers had to be taken care of too. Anaktuvuk, like any other village, had its neighborhood feuds. In fact, with their isolation where it was impossible to take off for another village once in a while to shake a bad case of cabin fever, they probably had more occasion to squabble. So, as a result, two of the fellows had complaints to make to the Commissioner at Kotzebue against neighbors who had crossed them or violated village rules. On rare occasions, bush planes would fly to Anaktuvuk during

111

the winter and land on the ice, and the complainers always hoped they could build a case sufficient to bring forth the United States Marshall.

"You know," Marvin warned them, "once you make this complaint, you can't change your minds. Maybe by the time you go back home you won't be mad at this man any more. Then if the Marshall comes, what would you do?"

"Oh, we got ba-a-ad man up there!" one of them insisted, and the other nodded his head vigorously in agreement. "He make plenty trouble for every people. We think maybe he's not right in his head."

So the complaints were filled out and mailed to Kotzebue. Whatever became of the situation from there on, we never knew.

The next order of business was to fill out vital statistic reports to send to the Kotzebue Commissioner. We filed statements of marriages, births, and deaths. One man who didn't make the trip to Shungnak sent this note to us:

Unknown Dear Friend Kobuk Teacher
    Just the drop a few lines to you by Clint. And I was thinking to get medician for my blood pressure because I am alway had skin disease every in summer. I hed that 3 or 4 years and if you have a any Medicene for that Please send me by Clint or by John Morry Akurad and send me a Standard Certificate berth of childs. No one told me before about it around here. and I have 3 children one gone a come this summer. If you send me the affidivet I can filled up here

Be good luck
I am very truly
Sam James

    P.S. I never go to school in my life and I think pretty hard to read it.

For one who had never had the advantage of formal schooling, Sam James did a beautiful job of getting his thoughts across to us. Eskimos write unusually good letters—uninhibited, frank, and expressive. This one from Sam we treasured, and did our best to comply with his requests.

Kayak loaded, ready for trip to fish camp.

Men's kayak race.

Robert Cleveland building a boat.

A boat-builder lays his ground work.

Far right - Charlie Sheldon, who was the first to greet us when we landed at Kobuk. (He has been dead for several years now.)

The only covered boat in the village.

Barge from Kotzebue coming into Shungnak.

A young fellow with his slingshot.

Going down the Kobuk, enroute to jade-hunting grounds.

Hiking across the tundra near Axel Knoll.

Staking jade claims required writing some descriptions.

Ted Tronsted, an old miner up on Dahl Creek above Kobuk, with a piece of raw jade.

A family and their fish-drying racks.

Cutting up salmon.

Cooking on a homemade stove.

Skidding a raft of logs up the river bank.

Whipsawing lumber.

Whipsawing lumber.

Building a cabin.

A good deal of bartering went on for a few days before the Arctic boys got underway to Kobuk. There was much swapping of oogruk (skin from the big bull seal), caribou leg skins to use in making mukluks, and sinew. Robert came to work one morning immensely pleased with himself.

"I sure make good trade last night," he bragged. "I get white mountain sheep skins one of those Arctic boy fellows. Pretty soon you see my wife he make me new parky."

Several days after their arrival, the Arctic boys hooked up their teams and moved on toward Kobuk. Their furs for commercial marketing all went to the trader's store—mink, marten, lynx, and fox. Except for the cash they needed to send their mail orders, they didn't deal in money. Cash was worthless at Anaktuvuk. Everything was barter. To see what sort of things they piled on their sleds for the return trip north was an education. Coffee was too bulky, so they took tea instead. They bought as many of the staple foods as they could carry that would not be damaged by either freezing or thawing, and a new supply of pocket combs. If there was money left over, each man chose for himself a choice knife or new gun and some ammunition, and a five-yard length of bright calico for the woman in his house to make into a new parka cover.

Back at Shungnak for one last night, a farewell party, and a rehashing of the local news picked up at Kobuk, and the next morning they hitched up their teams to head for home. The villagers walked with them to the top of the hill and stood there waving good-by, wishing them well, and exchanging little hilarities in Eskimo that brought forth mountains of laughter until their voices finally faded into the distance. For many days after that, the main topic of conversation revolved around the events of the visit and the anticipation of the next one.

CHAPTER XIV

BREAK-UP TIME

Except for an occasional dog team trip to Kobuk, we hadn't been anywhere we couldn't go on foot since we moved to Shungnak. Marvin's dream was to get on the river and explore the country. The only boat we had was a flat-bottomed little character almost as wide as it was long. Robert and Marvin spent their spare minutes all winter in the basement ripping it apart and extending it by about three feet. So come spring, we had a fifteen foot boat in which to start our travels.

As soon as the sun returned and the snow melted enough to permit, we dragged our prize down to the river and dressed it up with a few coats of paint—yellow on the outside and bright red inside. Flip, our little golden cocker spaniel pup the Collinses had given us, was our constant helper, though we'd have made more progress without him. We ended up with more paint on him than we had on the boat. And since all proper boats must have names, we named ours Flip I—Flip the First.

Norma Larkin was a delightful little waif who followed

at our heels all summer as close as Flip did. She lived at the far end of the village with her ailing mother, her grandmother, and little brother.

Because of the mother's poor health and the grandmother's age, the family was ill-prepared to make themselves a decent living. They had neither dog team nor boat. So when other families with menfolk moved out every spring to set up headquarters in their various fishing spots, Norma and her kin stayed in the village. They set their ragged little gill net in the river in front of their house all summer long and captured what few fish strayed into it.

Norma was a pretty little girl, about nine, bubbly and friendly, and one of our best students. She was up and waiting for us every morning as soon as we began to stir around, just to be sure she didn't miss anything. So of course she was standing by when we put the final touches on our new boat and I finished it off with the name we had given it.

I had scarcely lifted my brush off the last letter when Norma said, "F-L-I-P-I—Flip Eye!"

From that minute on, our boat was called the Flip Eye. No one every asked us how such a name came to be.

Just as the river had frozen in stages in the fall, so it broke up in the spring. By April, the sun was high enough in the sky for its daytime warmth to begin taking effect. Snow in the high country was melting and trickling in rivulets down into the many tributaries that filled the Kobuk. Each day the rivulets grew, and by May were pouring tons of water into the mother stream. As the river swelled, it broke loose the ice along its banks. And while the wild water was ripping up the ice from underneath, the sun was beating it into honeycomb from above. Inevitably, winter finally gave way to spring, and the ice crumbled and broke, moving a few inches or a few feet at a time. The movements were most apt to come between noon and mid-afternoon when the sun was warmest; but toward evening temperatures dropped rapidly and the shifting ice froze against its neighbor ice and stood still waiting for another day and the sun again. Each day the sun stayed with us longer and the hours of freezing were less. This was the time of year when we all spent most of our day and even our nights close to the river so we wouldn't miss that breathtaking few minutes known as the time "when the ice went out."

Irene Douglas and the old man, Kopotuk, reminded us constantly of the impending event.

"Better you stay down here all time," Kopotuk would say. "Any time ice go now. Anybody want to see, they stay here by river all day and all night."

"But the ice won't go out at night when it's cold, will it?" we'd ask, looking for an excuse to seek the warmth of our house when the evenings grew chilly.

"Never can tell," Irene warned. "I remember lots times when ice goes in night. Sun shines too long now. Ice never rests."

Late one afternoon in the last week of May, it finally happened. There were loud cracking and crashing noises from along the shore, and underneath the whole mass of jammed and broken ice cakes that still covered the river. The ice seemed to push from both sides. It heaved in the center, piling up hills of itself that tumbled over the hills ahead of them. As fast as one piece piled on top of another and left an open spot of water behind it, that spot was filled by another ice cake. The river water now had walls of ice to push against, and its work was soon done. With heaves and groans and crashes, the ice moved forward in masses, picking up speed as it rolled along. The masses that managed to stay in the mainstream kept moving out, but those that were squeezed to the side were grounded in the shallow water near shore and eventually thrown up onto the bank, forming walls of ice blocks as big as our kitchen. These ice walls melted slowly, and the remains of some of them were still in evidence a month later.

Most of the residents had moved out to spring fish camps while the ice was still solid enough for dog teams, so there was only a handful of us left to celebrate break-up time. Little Norma, and old Kopotuk, and all of us in between danced and shouted and waved our hands in ex-

133

citement, ushering in a summer in the Arctic and a new mode of travel—the waterway.

"Time to soak up my boat," Irene said happily.

"Ya! Ya!" agreed Kopotuk.

"Time to soak up my boat, too!" Marvin chimed in. For days, stray ice cakes and sometimes whole ice islands that nearly filled the river kept floating by. Then for hours at a time, the river would be almost clear. During one of these lulls we made our maiden voyage with the Flip Eye, and our neighbors who had stayed at home were on hand to see how it would perform. The river people are mighty boat-conscious, and there is much competition among the builders. Marvin clamped our ten-horse Johnson outboard motor to the stern of the boat, slid his shotgun under his seat, and with Flip and me settled in the passenger seat, zoomed down river for our first ride on the Kobuk. Flip loved it, and from then on our boat never got away from shore without him. He'd stand on the deck at the bow with his nose pointed into the wind, his hair blown back from his face, and his ears flapping.

The ducks were flocking north and season was officially closed; but to hungry Eskimos and hungry white men who hadn't seen a piece of fresh meat for months, that wasn't taken into consideration. We explored a small tributary below the village and flushed out two ducks in the brush along the bank. Marvin grabbed his gun and dropped one of them into the water. This was Flip's first and last lesson in retrieving. The gun shot sent him under the deck as far as he could go, and he didn't show face until long after Marvin had hauled in his own duck and started home.

Supper that night was long to be remembered. Marvin butchered our lone bird outside the back door, and I raced out to the steps when I heard him give a wild shout.

"Look! An egg! A real egg, shell and all. And a whole bunch of smaller ones!" He held out a handful of eggs in all stages of development, from the hard-shelled one to a soft-shelled one, and then a half dozen yellow yolks.

I shook my head. "We haven't seen a fresh egg since last fall. I've almost forgotten what they look like!"

I very carefully fried our hard-shelled egg in butter in my little one-egg frying pan, cut it in two, and we each had one bite. Then we boiled the rest of the egglets with the giblets for our breakfast the next morning.

CHAPTER XV

THE BOAT WRECK

Whether it was the taste of the egg or the feel of the river under our boat that set our blood boiling, I don't know; but the next day we decided to take our first trip upriver. Our craft classes had a whole boxful of nut cups, birch baskets, and miniature snowshoes and sleds to be mailed to our office in Juneau, where they would be sold. Since the post office was at Kobuk, this gave us a good reason to make our trip.

Robert and his wife Flora had set up two sawhorses on the river bank in front of their house and were building themselves a small fishing boat. It was still in the rib stage and lying upside down on the sawhorses. Robert was swaying steadily back and forth, a small plane held firmly in his hand slicing off curls of wood along a rib, while Flora held the boat steady. He stopped work and watched us intently as we untied the Flip Eye and loaded our gear into it.

"Where you going?" Robert asked in some astonishment.

"Up to Kobuk to the post office," Marvin told him. "Can't waste a beautiful day like this!"

"You see ice cakes out here yet?" Robert nodded toward the river. "Too much high water yet. Too much ice. I think you wait one more day."

"Oh, pshaw! You're just getting too old, Robert. Old man stay home—young man go to Kobuk!" With a wave of his hand, he dismissed Robert's protests.

We laid an extra motor in the bottom of the boat just in case we had trouble with the first one, and Marvin tossed in his hip boots. We considered ourselves well-equipped. This was to be a social call as well as a business trip, so we dressed in our best clothes. Marvin wore his down jacket and fur slippers I had given him for Christmas. I was by now sporting my caribou parka with the wolverine ruff and a new pair of rabbit-fur lined slippers. Under all this I was well covered with my longjohns because, even with the sun shining, it was cold on the river.

We were in high spirits that beautiful morning when we set out for Kobuk, smashing head on into soft remains of ice blocks, and ducking jauntily around those that were still firm and sharp and dangerous.

A mile above the village, the Kobuk branches—the larger branch going on up river, and the smaller we assumed being a tributary coming from we didn't know where. We had walked past this fork on every trip to the CAA station the past winter, and always wondered what it looked like around the first bend. Now we decided to find out.

The first curve only urged us to find what was around the next one. But after a half mile of this, we knew we shouldn't venture too far off our route; so Marvin shut off the motor.

"No point in burning gas right now," he explained. "We may as well drift back to the mainstream."

Outboards are some of the noisiest things in the world, so this was another new adventure—drifting on the Kobuk listening to the rush and tumble of giant river waters and the smashing of ice cakes meeting head on, vieing for survival. The cakes seemed to be getting thicker, and Marvin suddenly realized something strange was happening to us.

"What's wrong here, Lou? We aren't floating back to the main river the way we intended to. We seem to be going upstream further into this tributary!"

"That's not possible," I insisted. Boats don't drift upstream!"

"I know it isn't, but just watch that shoreline for a few minutes and see what's happening!"

I had to agree with him we were going the wrong way.

Marvin was never one to waste time in making decisions. "We'd better get out of here quick!" he snapped, and grabbed for the pull rope.

With his first yank, the motor started, and went racing like a madman out of control. It sounded as though it were ready to throw itself into a million pieces. Marvin pulled the head of the motor toward him to lift the bottom end out of the water—and sure enough, just as we had feared, the propeller blade was gone!

We were in serious trouble. Ironically, we had a standby motor lying in the boat, but we didn't have a second propeller. And Marvin was so sure those motors were going to get him where he wanted to go, that we didn't have a paddle either.

Above the crossribs on the bottom of the boat were four or five long boards going lengthwise of the craft with wide cracks between them for water drainage. These boards formed the floor we walked on.

"Get your feet up off the floor, quick!" Marvin ordered.

I tucked my feet under me and gripped both sides of the boat in a panic.

He ripped up one of the floor boards, and using it as a paddle, began to fight his way to shore. The ice cakes were a real menace now. We couldn't maneuver fast enough to avoid them, and hard ones as well as soft crashed against the boat. Every minute was taking us further from the Kobuk. We were caught right in the middle of a big bend in the river; and since the current naturally hugged the outside of the curve, that was the only way we could go. Never could we fight the current in two directions at once.

By the time we finally reached the bank, we were in the worst spot possible. The bank went straight up for six or seven feet, and the current hugging the shore was bringing with it monstrous chunks of ice that crashed into us unmercifully. Marvin's lips were tight and his black eyes snapping. I knew what that meant. Nothing was to be taken lightly. In times of a crisis such as this, he dictated, and I obeyed.

As best he could, he held the boat against the bank.

"Get out as quick as you can now!" he ordered.

I hesitated, appalled at the height of the bank above me.

"Get out, I said! Do something. Start crawling, jump, grab, whatever, but do it quick!"

This meant that I had to jump as high as possible and grab a firm handful of the tough grass at the top of the bank. I jumped and grabbed, but whatever it was I had in my hand let loose, and I fell back with clods of dirt and grass falling into my face. A second jump brought no better results.

"Get out of this boat, I told you!" Marvin shouted, and with my third jump I held on to something that didn't give way. I braced my feet against the wall of dirt in front of me and pulled myself to the top of the bank.

The half inch rope we used to tie our boat with was for some reason fastened to the side halfway between bow and stern, about the worst place in the world for it to be; but there it was. Marvin tossed the loose end up to me. I gave it one turn around a small aspen close to the bank, and held on with both hands.

This freed Marvin for a few minutes at least from bracing the boat against the bank with his improvised paddle. But just then an ice cake caught the bottom of the boat and ripped loose a four inch board. Water gushed in the full length of the boat on either side of the loose board. Marvin snatched up a two-pound coffee can we carried with us and began to bail. Obviously ours was a losing battle, so he dropped the can long enough to grab the dog and toss him up on to dry land with me. Then another few wild seconds of bailing to keep the boat afloat, and this time he tossed up the motor lying on the bottom of the boat. So it went until he had cleared the boat of the second motor, the box of craftwork, his hip boots, and gun. Each time something was tossed, I had to take one hand off my rope in order to grab it and keep it from falling back into the river; and each time I lost a few inches.

Now we were experiencing more difficulties because of the stupid way our boat was tied. With the tie rope halfway between front and back, the boat turned broadside against the oncoming current and ice cakes. This created a wall for ice cakes to crash against four or five times as wide as it would have been had the rope been tied to the end of the boat. And of course this meant more pressure that I was having to pull against.

I was within inches of the end of my rope; even with my foot braced against the base of the tree, and with both hands pulling, I was still losing ground.

"Marvin, get out of the boat—please!" I screamed at him. "I'm losing it! I can't hang on any longer!"

Marvin boomed back at me. "This is a government boat. We don't dare lose it. If you can't hang on, let go and I'll pile it up on the ice cakes down below!"

I didn't want to hear any more, and kept shouting, "No, no, no!" at the top of my voice.

The boat by this time was a quarter filled with water, and I had about four inches of rope left. It looked as though the game was about up when Marvin dropped the coffee can, and in a few seconds had untied his end of the rope. The boat shot forward; but Marvin made a lunge at the same time, slipped the end of his rope around a brace at the bow of the boat, and fastened it. In that split second while the rope was being transferred, I felt a bit of slack. A quick tug gave me just enough to wrap it around my hand a second time. This time, believe me, I hung on. Had the rope cut my hands in two, I don't think I would have let it slip again.

Now the boat was parallel to the bank and the pressure

decreased. Marvin didn't spend any more time bailing, but with one long leap he got two handfuls of tough grass and climbed to the bank.

"Robert told us not to come," he admitted grudgingly.

I'd been thinking the same thing, but I hadn't intended to say it.

CHAPTER XVI

THE WET WAY HOME

The willows along the riverbank were as thick as the trunks of banyon trees gone out of control, and almost as impossible to work our way through. But about a city block upstream the bank lowered and sloped onto a small, flat area. There we knew we had to dock our boat. With four hands on the rope, we worked through the maze of willows, and an hour later landed the boat on dry ground. My rabbit fur slippers were soggy wet and stretching so much they were falling off my feet. We used the pull rope from the motor to tie one of them on my foot; but in order to keep the other on, I had to curl my toes down with every step. Already, we were a mass of scars and cuts.

The logical route home seemed to be to follow the river at a safe distance from the water, although we knew we would end up across the river from the village. Marvin took the lead. The river was at flood stage, and every low spot that normally would have been dry had become a full-fledged tributary pouring melted snow from the surrounding area into the river. They were far too deep to wade, so Marvin had to build a bridge across each one. We'd look for the nearest fallen log and drag it to the edge of the water, then he would stand it up on end and let the top end drop across to the other side. If Marvin made it across the log without mishap, we'd send Flip next, and I went last. The logs were slippery and Flip was ecstatic with the excitement of it all; so invariably he never made it past the middle of a log before he slipped off into six or eight feet of ice water and had to be hauled out.

Improvising one bridge after another was exhausting us, so we decided to try another technique. Walls of ice cakes had been piled up along the river bank just as they had at the village, and these banks were rotting in the sun. They still seemed to have quite a bit of body to them, so might make a better route for us. Most of the flood stage tributaries had tunneled under this bank of ice to enter the river, and we hoped to be able to walk across the tops of these tunnels. That was a bigger disaster than bridge-building. Every few steps, we would hit an ice cake just ready to disintegrate. These honeycombed cakes were nothing but a mass of icicles held tightly together. When we put a foot into the middle of one, the icicles fell apart in all directions, and we would be staring into the open water beneath.

Now we had to choose a third method of attack. The stretch of the Kobuk from Shungnak to the Y, and the right leg of the Y that we were on should form the sides of a squat triangle. If we moved out through the woods in the general direction of the village, our route should make the third side of this triangle, and actually be the shortest route home. So off we started again into the spruce, free of the horrible willow brush that lined the river bank.

The ground underfoot was mushy and wet, and I was having problems with my loose slipper. Marvin was faring a little better because he had hip boots. The further inland we went, though, the mushier it got underfoot; and finally the mush became a complete cover of water. Within half an hour I was up to my knees in overflow, my feet freezing. Marvin by this time was carrying the dog; and considering the slippery, wiggly mess the little fellow had become, that was no simple matter. So at this point, Marvin decided to drop anchor and review the whole situation. This meant his having to climb the tallest tree we could find to have a look around. With hip boots on, that wasn't easy, but climb he did; and to his amazement he discovered we were on an island completely surrounded by water.

"Well, at least we know now why the water back there seemed to be flowing in the wrong direction," he called down to me. "That water we were on wasn't a tributary at all. I can see now that the Kobuk divides into two arms back there at the Y. The main river goes around one side of this island and the smaller arm goes around the other. Looks as though they meet again a couple of miles below the village."

"Is this good or bad?" I called back.

"Well, at least we know the lay of the land. I can see the village right across the island here. But migosh, there's nothing but water ahead. From here to the village is a regular lake!"

Our sloppy trek went on. By the time I was waist deep in water, Marvin was in worse shape than I. The water was pouring into the tops of his boots, and since there was nowhere it could go, he had to add two bootfuls of cold water to his load. The deeper the water, the more current it was able to conjure up. We were near exhaustion, and I was beginning to panic. I knew that the water dripping down my face had an occasional taste of salt in it.

Marvin sensed my state of mind. "Want me to piggy back you for a while?"

"Marvin, I feel like a quitter—but I just can't walk any farther in this stuff."

So with Flip in his arms and me on his back, he plodded on, one slow uncertain step at a time with two bootfuls of water.

Once we passed the mid part of our island, the water began to lower, and finally Marvin was able to unload the dog and me and empty his boots. We were sure now that we had it made, and then ahead of us we saw one more river of flood water, wider than any we had crossed before. We estimated twenty feet from one side to the other, and we couldn't find a fallen log long enough to span it. But about two-thirds of the way across, sticking out of the water, was a small stump about eight inches in diameter with two sturdy saplings sprouting up from the root. Marvin dropped the longest log he could find into the water, but its far end fell about six feet short of the stump. He eased out to the end of the log, jumped that six foot span to the stump, and then with one more jump, landed on the other side of the stream.

"You won't be able to jump from the log to the stump like I did," he said, "so jump as far as you can and grab one of those saplings and hang on!"

I curled up my toes to form little hooks and inched my way along. The end of the log was under water, slippery, and bouncing up and down, so I didn't waste any time there. I gave the longest jump I could and grabbed for the sapling. But what I didn't know was that Flip was right behind me. He jumped just as I did, and he got the stump. I had nowhere to put my foot, and I had probably grabbed the sapling a little too high anyway. It began to bend in my direction, while I was blindly kicking my feet hoping to find somewhere to put them. All I could think of was the fact that Marvin had told me to grab the sapling and hang on. So hang on I did until it let me right down on my back in the middle of the icy water. I went completely under, new parka, longjohns, and all.

Marvin made the statement of the day, and I never let him forget it—"Oh, Lou, you fell in!" He jumped back into the stream and dragged me out.

All the way across the island, I'd been thinking about those poor people who rode the old truck from Oklahoma to California in the *Grapes of Wrath,* and I felt a part of them. After every catastrophe or failure, I was sure we had reached rock bottom and nothing worse could possibly happen. But like the Joad family, we always found a new rock bottom. Sitting there in a heap on the edge of that last fatal flood stream, with my longjohns and fur parka sticking to me like cold slime, I knew this had to be the lowest of the rock bottoms. Either that or we were just so tired we didn't care any more. Whatever it was, Marvin sat down beside me and we laughed until we cried.

* * *

Seven hours after we left Shungnak that morning, we finally came in sight of it again. The few people who remained in the village had heard us shouting to one another all the way across the island. They were waiting on shore for us. Irene and three other women pushed a thirty foot river boat into the water; and weaving in and out around the pieces of ice still floating downstream, came to our rescue. They put forth their best efforts to take our whole situation seriously, but it was useless.

Irene said in her saddest voice, "I'm so sorry!" Then she plopped her hand over her mouth to hide a giggle, but we could hear her "tee hee's" slipping out through her fingers. I'm sure we two cheechakos were the brunt of all the village jokes for the rest of the day and for many days to come.

The next morning the river was miracuously clear of ice, and flood waters had receded. Robert was at our door waiting when we finally got out of bed.

"We take my big boat up today and get yours," he announced.

"You can't get my boat in yours!" Marvin laughed.

"I think so. Easy. My boat thirty feet long. Carry lots load."

Marvin was happy to accept the offer, but wasn't convinced that this was the time to go.

"Maybe we should wait until the water goes down a little, Robert."

Robert chuckled. "Water already go down. Only about one day from flood time until all flood water is down."

"You mean if we'd sat there overnight with that boat, we could have walked home with no trouble?"

"Maybe!" The twinkling eyes told us that in this case, "maybe" meant "yes."

So Robert and Marvin went back to the scene of our accident, loaded the smashed-up Flip Eye and all our gear into the river boat, and brought it home.

I wondered if Marvin had been feeling a little guilty over this whole affair, and sure enough he had.

"You know," he admitted, "I must have forgotten to put a cotter key on the end of that propeller blade. Otherwise it couldn't have fallen off."

I found out in the years to come that this was the way it would always be with Marvin. He was rash enough to get us into these messes and then smart enough to get us out.

CHAPTER XVII

EVERYDAY SURVIVAL

The Arctic was the best spot in the world to challenge one's ability to have the nicities of life. Just plain survival was relatively simple, as evidenced by the fact that many of us lived there. But first class survival took a little more effort.

For instance, there was the bread. That first year I had a bitter struggle with my sourdough pot. I still hadn't learned the art of feeding my starter every few days, and little by little its strength was diminishing. Had I added a spoonful of warm water and a bit of flour once in a while, my starter could be with me still; but I was quite unenlightened. The day came when I mixed up a batch of brown bread and nothing happened. The starter was stone dead. My sponge got colder and crustier as the day wore on. Finally, in desperation I pushed four hard little loaves into the oven and hoped for the best. An hour later the best was four brown lumps that felt like rocks. Even Flip gave me a sad, apologetic glance, and walked away from them. I could have taken them down the hill where any of the hungry sled dogs would have gulped them down without asking questions; but I was ashamed to admit I had ever produced them, so the bread finally went the route of some of my other mistakes. From the back step, I heaved one loaf at a time, as far as I could. With the weight of lead, they disappeared into the moss.

With the demise of our sourdough starter, we were reduced for several weeks to Sailor Boy pilot bread. There were no fresh potatoes to use in fermenting some new starter.

The solution to our problem came from an unexpected source in the form of the traveling nurse. Good old Keaton! Mildred Keaton, her full name was, but few people knew it. To most of us she was Keaton. It wasn't said with lack of respect, but rather in a tone of admiration the way we say Washington or Lincoln.

Keaton was a good-sized, well-built lady somewhere in middle age. It didn't matter much where. She had been a nurse with the Indian Service for many years, had traveled all over Alaska by any means available—dog team, boat, snowshoe, and airplane. In earlier days she had mushed the Arctic coast from Barrow to Demarkation Point peddling pills, pulling teeth, and giving shots. Once a year she made the run up the Kobuk, riding the mail plane from Kotzebue to Selawik, Noorvik, Kiana, Shungnak, and Kobuk. I'm not sure how she managed her work in the villages lower down, but when she arrived at Shungnak, she unloaded her gear and the plane went on to Kobuk without her. The mail pilots always overnighted with Ray Chaplain at Kobuk and started the return trip from there the next morning. This gave everyone a chance to answer any mail he might have received the day before and get it in the pouch.

Mid-winter was with us, and Keaton hadn't had any supper when she arrived. I was torn between two fires. We hadn't had mail for a month, so the mailbag held priority over everything else. Should I let the letters from home go unopened while I prepared supper for our guest, or should I let her wait until I had taken a hasty glance at part of my mail at least?

Keaton answered the question without my having to ask it aloud. "I always get my own meal when I come in on the mail plane," she said. "The teachers are busy reading their mail."

"You're sure you don't mind?" I asked apologetically.

"I wouldn't know how to act if it were otherwise," she said simply.

She peeled off her outdoor gear—tall fur mukluks, big mitts, and a huge gray fur parka. The parka seemed heavy when she lifted it off her shoulders, and I noted that she laid it down carefully. As she draped it over the back of a chair, the inside was exposed, and there across the back of it sewed into the lining was a band full of pockets resembling an ammunition belt. Nearly every slot had a small bottle in it. She must have noted my curiosity.

"My serums," she explained. "It's the only way I have of keeping them from freezing—wear them right inside my parka."

But more astounding was the bulge in one of the pockets—much larger than the serum bottles.

"What's that?" Marvin asked her.

"Oh, that's some sourdough starter the teacher down at Kiana gave me. Our yeast foam all got wet last fall when Archie's barge was lightering it off the *North Star* at Kotzebue, and we haven't had any decent bread at the hospital all winter. I'll bet those cooks will be glad to see this!"

"Keaton," I said, "you're not going to get out of here with all that. You've got a whole pint and you don't need that much!"

The next morning Keaton had only half a jar of starter to take back with her. I had the other half. I never let my starter go dead again. For the rest of the three years we spent at Shungnak, we had big, fat, moist loaves of bread.

Where that wonderful lady got all her energy, I don't know. Once the shourdough starter had been divided and

151

her supper taken care of, Mildred Keaton rolled up her sleeves, set up her medicine bag in one of the classrooms, and rang the bell. Up the hill came the villagers—young and old, big and small, the halt and the lame and the husky. They settled themselves in seats or on the floor and waited as each one took his turn to see the nurse. She gave shots, pulled teeth, weighed, rubbed, punched, scolded, praised, or did whatever had to be done to heal their aches and pains. She dished out pills along with good advise and never closed her medicine case until the wee hours of the morning. Then she quietly tiptoed into our living quarters and to bed without waking us. Next morning she was the first one up and dressed, had her sleeping bag, medicine case, and serums all bundled up and waiting when the mail plane arrived. The villagers gathered on the river to bid her good-by. We wouldn't see her again for a year, but as soon as the plane faded into the gray of that winter day, we were already counting the days until she would be back again.

* * *

With the return of the sun after a dreary, dark winter, Marvin took a long look at the battered old greenhouse attached to the house at the end of the classrooms.

"With a little fixing on that greenhouse," he said, "we'll not only have good bread. We'll have some fresh vegetables, too."

Every day after school he was busy pounding, sawing, and rebuilding what was left of the greenhouse into a neat little garden area that could hold in the heat of the sun. In it we planted all sorts of promising looking little seeds and babied them along with love and care such as we had never given a garden in our lives before. As soon as school was out in May, we dug up an outdoor garden spot back of the school.

By mid-June we were relatively safe from killing frosts, so transplanted most of our greenhouse plants. I remember especially the two hundred delicate little carrots we dug up carefully so as not to destroy the tiny roots. We jabbed holes in the ground deep enough to accommodate the long center root without its having to be bent, and patted dirt carefully around each little carrot. We were proud of our cabbage, the biggest and sturdiest plants we had.

Norma Larkin, left to play by herself most of the summer when other children moved out of the village, was at our heels from morning until night as the garden progressed. We spent time with every new planting to explain to her what vegetable we had and what it would look like when it ripened.

"Norma is showing a lot of interest in this garden," Marvin noted. "The poor little kid sure doesn't have anything at home to give her any incentive, so this is a good thing for her. What do you think of the idea of giving her some kind of reward so she realizes that you can gain something by showing some initiative?"

"I think we should. How about letting her have a little garden of her own?"

"Up here by ours, you mean? No, she wouldn't stick with it when it came to carrying water up the hill. She might as well have it down at the river."

So when the cabbage were ready to transplant, I said in a big-hearted way, "Norma, we're going to give you a cabbage plant for your very own. You can plant it at the corner of your house down by the river and water it every day."

I went on about the wonders of her cabbage plant and how good it would taste when her grandma cooked it.

She listened intently and in complete silence through my entire pep talk, and I felt like a real benefactor. Then as an afterthought, I asked, "Do you want a cabbage?"

"No," she said simply.

Marvin and I stood speechless as our little visitor, suddenly disinterested in the gardening, turned and tripped merrily down the hill.

"What do you think of that?" I asked, quite piqued.

"We won't press the issue," Marvin decided. "Somewhere along the way there's still a missing link—I don't quite know where it is. She has seen teachers grow gardens, but she's never seen her own family do it. In fact, when you think of it, Irene is the only one in the village who grows a garden. Norma somehow just doesn't relate to the idea of having a garden herself any more than she thinks of going into a classroom to teach. Those are two jobs that only the teacher does."

For the next two months we made a dozen trips a day to our garden, carried buckets of water, and gloried over every inch of growth. Norma occasionally trailed along with us, but never offered to carry a pail of water.

Any time after the first of August we could get our killing fall frosts, so each day we kept our fingers crossed and hoped for a little more time before we had to harvest.

One of those days when we were on borrowed time, Marvin noted two little parka-clad forms bobbing up and down between the rows of greenery. Bounding out the back door, we were just in time to see Norma and a little girl playmate whose family had come back to the village the day before, walking down the middle of our garden pulling up carrot, celery, and turnip plants and piling them into their arms. We had never in all our years of teaching upended a youngster and given him a good paddling, but it happened then—right in the middle of the turnip patch. Then we stood by like a couple of old ogres and made those scared little girls punch holes and replant every vegetable they had uprooted.

Once they had scooted out of sight, of course, we pulled all the replants and ate them for supper that night.

"I guess there's more than one missing link!" blustered Marvin, "and I don't even know where to start looking for it. For some reason, I didn't expect this of Norma, especially when you think that she wasn't even willing to grow a cabbage of her own!"

The rest of the garden had to be harvested shortly thereafter. Actually, none of it amounted to much. Our mothers back in Wisconsin would have tossed vegetables of this size to the pigs and chickens; but when you haven't had a bite of greenery or fresh vegetables for a year, you aren't going to throw anything away. Our two hundred little carrots were the most interesting of our harvest. They hadn't grown much since they left the greenhouse, but at least they had changed shape. None was any bigger than my little finger at the top end; and every one, after going down for about two inches, had made a right angle turn and grown parallel to the ground. Permafrost was so close to the surface, they couldn't go any further and were trying to find their way back to the sun. But what they lacked in size, they made up for in goodness. They were almost clear enough to see through, and were so crisp they snapped like broken glass. They lasted for two meals and we never went to that great effort again to grow more another year. In fact, we didn't grow much of anything the next year. Our gardening venture took a back seat to more pressing things.

CHAPTER XVIII

OUR FIRST TRIP FOR JADE

We had heard stories about the jade at Shungnak before we ever reached the village. On our way enroute from Seattle in the fall of '45, we had stopped briefly in Juneau. The boat docked for a couple of hours in the middle of the night, but two of our supervisors from the Alaska Native Service office met our ship and took us uptown for a cup of hot chocolate at 3 A. M. Our hasty conversation had touched on many topics, but I noted that it repeatedly went back to the subject of jade. There are several deposits along the upper Kobuk; and for many years the local natives had used it in limited amounts for toolmaking.

Although the jade closest to the village was up river about ten miles and then another five miles inland to Dahl Creek, the Shungnak people didn't hunt in that area. Two old Swedish fellows had mined both gold and jade there for years and were well established. So the villagers went instead down the Kobuk twenty miles, and then into the Shungnak River, a tributary that came into the Kobuk

157

from a northerly direction. Ten miles up the Shungnak, the flat country came to an end and rose sharply into hills that formed steep walls on either side. Out of this narrow gorge the river, though not a large one, tumbled in torrents onto the flats. At the mouth of the gorge floe rocks of jade, carried through the canyon by the force of the walled-in river, slowed and dropped down, either to the river bed or along the many beautiful bars.

Uncle Ralph Larrabee, my mother's bachelor brother, had gone north from Wisconsin to work in Fairbanks the spring of '46. So when summer blossomed to its fullest the first part of July, he flew to Shungnak to visit us. The village made him guest of honor at our Fourth of July celebration complete with boat and kayak races, and Lawrence Gray who by now was in charge of the reindeer herd, took him out onto the tundra one day to see the reindeer. But the frosting on the cake had yet to come.

"What would you think about a trip up the Shungnak to hunt for jade?" Marvin asked him.

"Just say when, and I'll be ready to go!" Uncle Ralph was thrilled at the very idea.

"Okay. I'll go down to the village right after breakfast and start recruiting," Marvin promised. "I don't think I'll have any trouble getting volunteers to go."

He didn't, and the next morning the village was a sea of bustle and activity as we loaded our gear and shoved off. Eight of us made the trip—Robert Cleveland and his two brothers, Johnny and Charlie, Robert's son-in-law, Teddy Jack, Nora Custer, Uncle Ralph, Marvin, and I. And of course Flip. We started out at noon in Robert's 30-foot river boat—the same one that had carried the Flip Eye home after our disastrous boat wreck the previous spring. We powered it with our ten-horse Johnson outboard from the school.

Those who remained behind lined the river bank to bid us good-by.

"Bring us back plenty jade! Maybe we get rich!"

"Mr. Warbelow, you make those old man work, and young man, too!"

"Marvin, ask Johnny 'bout fish. He have secret grayling place!"

They were still calling out all sorts of free advice when Marvin yanked the pull rope, and the roar of the motor drowned them out.

The trip down river our first twenty miles was perfect. The Kobuk is a swift river, so the motor purred along blissfully with never a threatening spit. If anyone in this world can relax, it's an Eskimo boating down river on a midsummer day. I can still see Nora, sitting at the rear of the boat in her dark blue calico parka with the hood back against her shoulders and her black braids sprinkled with bits of reindeer hair sliding down her back. Munching cold salmon eggs and dried caribou jerky, her mind a million miles away, she was as happy as any queen I have happened to know in my time.

Once we left the Kobuk and turned into the Shungnak, our troubles began. We spent six hours fighting our way from the mouth to our camping spot—about ten miles by river.

"It's going to be work every step of the way up this river," Marvin warned. "Everybody have your poles ready and jump in there quick when we need you!"

Each of us was equipped with a pole about eight feet long. Whenever the creek became so shallow and rocky that we couldn't operate the motor, all of us stood up and pushed along the river bottom with our poles.

Robert was keeping a close eye on me. "Lou, when you push, you careful you don't slip when boat move and fall out."

I anchored my feet a little further apart to let him know I was heeding his warning.

"First time I ever have chance to pole!" I replied, and it occurred to me that Marvin and I were sometimes slipping into the Eskimo style of putting our words together. The very thing Marvin had warned against.

"If we adopt the Eskimo lingo, they'll never learn proper English," he had reasoned.

But poling didn't always solve our problem. The boat

159

sometimes got hung up on rocks and riffles, or the water was so swift that the current pushed us back downstream. Whenever this happened and the boat came to a complete halt, Teddy and Charlie went into immediate action. They pulled their hip boot tops up to their fullest; and with tow lines fastened to either side of the boat, they jumped out. With one man on each side, they walked the banks and pulled with the ropes while the rest of us poled.

About noon we came to a spot where a slough joined the Shungnak.

"Marvin, better we stop here for coffee," Johnny called.

"What's the matter, Johnny—you all tired out already?" Marvin bantered.

"Oh, I tink good place to stop," Johnny returned, wagging his head up and down wisely.

He chose this spot for a reason. Our companions had been here before and knew what they were doing. While Teddy built a small fire of dried sticks and hung a black coffee pail over it, Johnny, Marvin, and I dropped our fishlines into the pool at the slough. Marvin managed to bring in two nice grayling; but Johnny, with a barbless hook he had made from a beaver tooth, pulled in twenty fish in a matter of ten minutes.

"How do you do it, Johnny?" Marvin asked in bewilderment.

Johnny dangled the hook in front of our noses, then stuffed it into his pocket for safekeeping.

"This kind hook only ting to catch grayling," he explained.

We stashed the fish for our next meal, and went on up river. By early evening we reached our campsite—a point of land that jutted out into the river about ten feet above the water. Axel Knoll, they called it. But Uncle Ralph was a little hard of hearing, so when some months later he sent us pictures he had taken, he labeled it Axel's Nose. The name fitted it quite well.

We pitched our tents side by side. Marvin, Ralph, and I had our own tent and food, but that night we all ate supper together—roast grayling that Robert had prepared.

Nora Custer, official cook, flips a pancake.

Marvin lights a pipe for an elderly lady.

Kobuk man showing Marvin how to snag driftwood floating down river by using a weight on a long string.

Reindeer roundup. Deer inside the corral.

Reindeer team takes a rest.

Norma Larkin who named the "FLIP EYE."

Sophie Cleveland and baby.

Clara Lee and her baby.

Pensive pre-schooler.

School girl and her dog.

Shungnak child.

General "Muktuk" Marston, founder of the Alaska Territorial Guard during World War II, visits Shungnak.

Uncle Ralph and Marvin at the grayling stream.

Three senior citizens from Kobuk.

Young lad tying the family boat to its anchor.

Wood sawing was a daily job.

Musher cooking his dog food.

He cut eight sturdy willow sticks, sharpened the ends, and on each stick he secured two grayling, head and all. Teddy by this time had his campfire going, so Robert stuck the willows into the ground in a circle around the fire with the top ends bending in to meet above the center of the flame. It made a perfect miniature wigwam. When the fish were cooked, each of us took a stick and ate our grayling off it like hot dogs at a wiener roast.

That was the best meal we cheechakos had for three days. I was a poor planner and an inexperienced camper, so the loaf of bread and cold salmon and other odds and ends I had packed were long gone before we ever reached home.

Our sleeping arrangement wasn't much better. All we had taken for bedding were two blankets and a sleeping bag that unzipped into a big flat blanket. With all our clothes on, we squeezed together on the bag with the blankets over us, and shivered the night away in complete misery.

"Are you sure this is all the bedding you brought?" Ralph asked once during the night.

When he was greeted with stony silence, he didn't ask again.

Morning brought sunshine and a beautiful day, so we soon forgot our woes of the night before. Ralph was up and around at his usual five o'clock rising time and woke up the whole camp. Our Eskimo friends had bedrolls of caribou skins and had evidently slept in perfect cozy comfort. We heard no complaints from them.

While we ate a cold breakfast in our tent, Nora busied herself over the fire making hotcakes and oatmeal mush. Her stove was a clever concoction of a circle of rocks around a small fire, with the top of a fifty gallon oil drum laid across the rocks to make a perfect stove top. Nora boiled up a kettle of oatmeal mush and set it aside. Then she soon had her big black skillet sizzling hot. She poured in enough batter to make a hotcake the size of the skillet, and carefully juggled it back and forth a few times to loosen it from the bottom when it was ready to turn. Then with one quick jerk, she flipped it three feet into the air.

It turned a somersault, and landed smack in the middle of the pan again. Her menfolk sat around on the ground, each with a tin plate and a big spoon. They devoured the kettle of mush without milk or sugar in time to take care of the hotcakes as they came off the griddle.

With breakfast over, everyone took to the river.

"Water is low," Robert noted. "That's good. Easy to cross. Easy to see jade."

Old Johnny viewed the river with skepticism.

"I dunno," he pondered. "Maybe too swift fo' old man. Maybe better I—"

"Ya-a-a! Johnny, ya-a-a!" chorused the rest of his group.

"You not too old when time for hotcakes!" Robert reminded him. "You get in water like all of us!"

So with everyone hooting in delight, Johnny gingerly picked his way to the river's edge.

In hip boots, shoepacks, or old mukluks, we walked the sandbars and hunted the river bottom for pieces of jade. Marvin and I wore parka covers of canvas with big pockets across the front where we stored our rocks. The jade was beautiful. It ranged in color from light apple green to near black, and in size from pebbles to rocks weighing twenty pounds or so. We found it scattered from the dry sand bars to the deepest parts of the river bed. Under water it looked even more green than it did when it was dry.

Most of the rocks had a green side and a mottled brown side. If the green side was turned up, the rocks were easy to locate; but the brown sides were elusive. We had to keep our eyes open to locate them. We were continually crossing the river in order not to miss any of the sand bars; and poor little Flip spent a good share of his time trying to swim the deep spots in a strong cross current. Our hip boots were tricky to handle. To get into water above the tops was worse than no boot at all because we ended up carrying a bootful of water. Or if we lifted a foot too high, the water underneath buoyed it up like a balloon.

Hunting was good that morning and my pocket was filling up fast. Before long the weight of the rocks was dragging me down and I found it harder and harder to keep my balance in the current. Finally I lifted a foot too high, the water pushed my boot up as though I had a giant spring under it, and I was upended. The day was hot and a good dousing didn't feel too bad, but my pride was injured.

Robert had told us stories about an old gold-mining camp up river about a mile toward the gorge, the remains of the Kobuk-Alaska Mining Company, now defunct. Ralph and Marvin were curious about it; so toward mid-afternoon, we all started working our way steadily up river, hunting jade as we went. We were exhausted by the time the mine came within sight, but Ralph wasn't so tired that he hadn't had the energy to scout the tundra along the way and pick a hatful of big, tart blueberries for supper.

What was left of the mine amazed us. The long sluice box still in good condition sat with its riffles empty of everything but dead leaves and a few twigs. Behind it was a frame building that housed a huge steam engine, just like new. I didn't know enough about mining to know why the engine was there in the first place. But I did know there was ten miles of tundra back to the Kobuk, and I wondered how they ever got a piece of equipment that size over it. Marvin was wondering the same thing.

"How did they get this thing out here in the first place?" he querried.

Johnny and Charlie, the older of the Cleveland brothers, had some knowledge of it.

"They get big crew from Kotzebue I think," Charlie began. "They bring it in with dead men."

"What do you mean—dead men?" I wanted to know.

I got a big laugh for my stupidity, but Charlie patiently explained.

"Dead man is big log. They tie long cable around middle of log, then dig hole in tundra and bury log. Other end of cable stick out. They use this cable to pull engine. When end of cable come, they have to dig more holes for more dead men."

"Didn't that engine just dig itself into the tundra instead of sliding?" Marvin wanted to know.

179

Johnny had been listening intently to his brother's story. "They have big—you know—whatchacallum—underneath."

"Skids?"

"Ya-a-a! Skids I tink."

"That must have taken a whale of a long time to dig all those holes. They'd have to be only a couple hundred feet or so apart."

"Ya-a-a," agreed Johnny. "I tink it take lo-o-ong time!"

The Kobuk-Alaska Mining Company had been financed by Outside money, and had gone bankrupt before the operation ever got off the ground. So there sat the monstrous equipment, patiently waiting for someone with enough initiative and imagination to get it out.

Our next day we hunted the river bottom close to camp on Axel Knoll. Johnny was played out from his first day on the river, so was more than willing to give his boots up to Uncle Ralph who had been tramping in shoepacks, and have himself a vacation for the day. Ralph was the second casualty of the expedition. He got into deep water and swift current, lifted a foot too high, and under he went, billfold, pocket watch, and all. We dried his paper money out as best we could, and threw away two rolls of film that had gone under with him. His watch never ran after that, but he insisted that didn't matter.

"It never ran before, either," he admitted.

By evening, we had stacked up three or four hundred pounds of raw jade along the bank and decided that was as much as the boat could handle. So next morning, after a starvation supper in our tent, and an even scantier breakfast, we broke camp and started home. I assumed that the trip down the Shungnak would be just a matter of letting the current do the work. But as usual, I was wrong. The bow of the boat had a habit of snagging on rocks in shallow places and being whirled around sidewise. So for a good share of the way, two men with long ropes had to walk the bank or wade the river and hold the boat back to slow its pace.

We stopped for coffee break at our grayling slough.

180

Ralph, an experienced fisherman, declared he wouldn't let Johnny get the best of a white man again.

"Let me use your fish pole this time, Marvin," he whispered with a wise little arch of his brow. "I'll show Johnny how to catch fish!"

"I wouldn't bet too much on that!" grinned Marvin, and handed over his tackle.

Johnny pulled in one fish after another; so Ralph, who got nothing, decided he would have to have Johnny's fishhook. But Johnny wasn't sure he wanted to sell it.

Next day while Marvin and Ralph were up river to check at the CAA station on Ralph's flight back to Fairbanks, Johnny came up to see me.

"I tink about that fishhook. Uncle Ralph want pretty bad. Only one I got, but he good to me, so I sell him for two dolla."

"You're out of your mind, Johnny!" I gasped. "No one would pay that kind of money for one little fishhook!"

Wrong again I was. Uncle Ralph went home next day with the beaver tooth in his pocket.

CHAPTER XIX

KOPOTUK

Kopotuk was one of the most fascinating persons we had ever known. When the missionaries came to the Arctic, they encouraged the native people to adopt white man type names for the sake of convenience, since in their own language each person had only one name. So names like Grey, Cleveland, Stringer, Black, and Carlson appeared; and each person had a first and last name in addition to his own Eskimo name. Kopotuk became Charlie Coffin, but he was one of the few villagers we called by his native name.

He was the oldest man in the village. No more than five feet tall, he had a shock of snow white hair that set off his black eyes and the leatherness of his dark skin; and he walked with a kink in his back. His was an expressive face, and he was a bundle of enthusiasm. One of the hardest workers in the village, he took his religion seriously, and was a top notch story teller. English was difficult for him and he was continually groping for words to express himself, so any communication between us went at a snail's pace. He came up the hill often to visit, and from him we learned some priceless Eskimo history.

He had been raised at Kalla, some distance up river. His childhood home was a true igloo made of chunks of sod much like the igloo we had in Shungnak. In the center of the room, directly under the seal gut window, Kopotuk's father dug a hole in the dirt floor. This was the family's fire pit. Whenever a fire was burning, the window was opened to let the smoke out; but as soon as the fire died down, the window was sealed shut again. Eskimos then, and even in the forties when I knew them, weren't lavish with their heat. The purpose for building their home partially underground was to add warmth; and their fur clothing they wore constantly in cold weather served as an insulator so they could be comfortable in an unheated cabin. Wood was not only sometimes hard to come by, but their homemade tools made wood cutting a slow and difficult job. With proper foresight, the native people seldom cut wood near their homes, and this necessitated hauling fire logs sometimes long distances by dog sled. Or for those who didn't have dogs, it meant pulling the sled themselves.

"My papa make his own stove, too," Kopotuk told us. "He find big tree and cut off stump maybe like this." He extended his hands to indicate a length of about two feet. "He hollow out one end of stump with chisel and set it down on floor like bowl."

"Where did you get a chisel?" Marvin wanted to know.

"Oh-h-h, my papa make. He find long, sharp stone and some wood for handle. Then he tie stone to handle with rope he make from caribou leather."

"When my mama get ready to cook, she fill hollow stump maybe half full water. She makes stones hot in fire pit and put in water. Then she put in some kind meat. Stones make water hot and meat cook."

"What kind of meat did you have, Charlie?"

"Oh, we have caribou sometime or moose or bear. Maybe in sometime grayling or whitefish. My papa make big plate like this outa wood." His hands formed an imaginary dish. "When meat finish to cook, my mama put pieces on dish. We all sit on floor and eat."

"No forks?" I asked.

He smiled and shook his head. "No—no fork. We eat with finger. My papa even make cup with wood too and we drink broth from hot meat."

Then Kopotuk told us how he and a boy from a neighboring family roamed the woods all summer picking berries and slingshotting at a variety of little ground and tree animals, or lolled on the river banks fighting off hoards of mosquitoes with smudges.

"That must have been a happy way to live," I remarked. "No school to worry about—no taxes!"

Kopotuk suddenly sat up straighter in his chair, his eyes snapping, and he said emphatically, "No. No happy."

In his halting, limited English, he made us feel that life had been boring and monotonous. It was a timeless thing with nothing but the seasons to break the monotony. Even the food, he said, offered no variety. The meat was saltless, and of course the broth. Beyond that they had not much more than berries and birds, and the greens they pulled from the river bottom to cook in the wooden pot.

Each spring Kopotuk's family loaded its meager belongings and caribou skins into the boat, with the dogs and a supply of dried meat, and set off for the long trip down the Kobuk River to its mouth at the village of Kotzebue.

"It take us long time, that trip. We always drift, and if water go slow, we go slow. My papa have paddles and some other kind long poles we use when we get stuck on sand bars and maybe if river carry us too close to bank, we can push off."

They passed by such spots as are now the villages of Kobuk and Shungnak, past the mouth of the beautiful Ambler River, and on down to Kiana and Noorvik, across big Kobuk Lake and finally to Kotzebue itself, the hub of the Arctic in that area.

"Every mans and families comes from every place all around to make summer in Kotzebue," he explained dra-

185

matically. "All the caribou peoples come from river villages like my own people come. From Noatak River and from Kobuk and any river. Then salt water Eskimos come from islands and from up coast and down coast. We bring our caribou skins and Salt Water people have lotsa pokes fresh seal oil and big piles sealskin rope. We make lotsa trade these peoples."

It was a gala time when the boatloads of families, tents, and dogs converged on the spit and began setting up temporary homes for the summer all along the shore and around the edges of the village. These summers were the happiest times of Kopotuk's young life, and he reminisced them tenderly. Each spring as old friends met, there was much shaking of hands, bouncing up and down and laughing, and dancing and singing among the elders before they settled down to the serious business of fishing for their winter's supply of food for themselves and the dogs.

While the grown-ups were renewing old acquaintances from previous years, the younger set was doing the same in a different fashion. Last year's playmates had grown a head taller and changed in appearance; the boys' voices that had been high pitched and childish just a few months before were deeper and a little uncertain with a cracking now and then. So they felt shy with one another and each stayed close to his own tent until curiosity finally overcame the shyness, and little by little they began to mingle and exchange short greetings. Then finally came the long, endless days of constant companionship and running over the tundra for berries or playing in the icy lines of water that rolled onto the beach from the great ocean.

Here Kopotuk saw his first white man. The whaling ships were plying the waters between Seattle and Barrow in quest of the long strips of the fabulous black baleen from the mouths of giant whales that made their homes in the Arctic Ocean at the top of the world. On the way north the ships stopped off at Nome and Kotzebue to do a bit of business on the side. Kopotuk remembered the day a whaling boat docked off the coast, and smaller boats brought the sailers to shore.

"These white mans from boat all look us. I see one

man come to me, and he have nice face to me, like smile. I see he have lo-o-ng beard, all white. Eskimo never see that kind before. He pat me on my head and say, 'My boy,' but I no call him Papa!"

He remembered, too, the first time he tasted salt, and the first match he struck. The salt came from the big ship. Probably his father had traded a few choice marten or mink skins for it and made it well worth the sailor's time to stay and barter. The matches that no doubt also came from the white man's ship were called Chinese matches. A whole box of matches had one solid head; and each match stick as it was broken from the mass, took a portion of the solid head with it—enough to spark a fire.

Summers in the Arctic are short, and winters come early. As the days began to shorten and the nights to chill, the Eskimo families pulled in their nets and folded them away until the next spring. Dried fish was tied in bundles and stored in the big boats along with the tents and cooking gear and the dogs and ropes. The caribou skins had been replaced by pokes of oil and twists of sealskin rope that would make snowshoes and lashings for their sleds when winter came. Then with many good bys, the families set off in their various directions for their winter homes.

The trip up river in the fall was a much slower and more difficult one than the ride down in the spring. It took the family six weeks to fight its way upstream by pushing with long poles against the river bottom near shore. Whenever the river bank was free of buckbrush, the men put some of the dogs ashore with long ropes tied to the boat and let them pull until the brush or willows crowded them out again. Snow usually found its way to their igloo at Kalla before the family did each fall, so the fire pit and the shelter of the four sod walls were a welcome sight. And with salt to season their meat and Chinese matches to light their fire, life became just two steps more pleasant.

The Kopotuk we knew in the 1940's was all of seventy years old and just beginning to receive his monthly old age pension checks of 25 dollars. He was an independent old fellow who still set his fish net every summer and ran a short trapline during the winter. So with his monthly check to supplement his few needs, he did very nicely. His cabin was old and no longer to his liking, so during the summer of '46, he started his new house.

Every morning he trudged in his own stooped little way with his arms swinging back and forth away from his body out to the wood cutting area where he harvested his logs for the small cabin he would build. When that part of his work was done, he lashed them together into a raft, floated them down the river to the village, and one by one rolled them up the bank to his cabin site. Why he chose a spot so close to the river we could not understand; but with the high water at breakup time lapping away at his very doorstep, he had to build a retaining wall across the whole front side. For this, he needed good sized boulders not to be found in the village; so up the hill he came one day to borrow the school wheelbarrow. He could haul only one rock at a time; and the trip to his source of boulders was either a long one or a rough one, because we never saw him bring in more than three rocks a day, even though he worked at it from morning until night.

The rocks were finally collected and cement mixed; and with help from about no one, Kopotuk completed his rock wall. We couldn't help but wonder why the young fellows who strolled aimlessly or napped at midday in their bunks didn't offer a hand.

The wheelbarrow didn't come back to the school until the rock wall was finished. Marvin was perturbed when he noted that the whole front edge was badly battered. Kopotuk wasn't one you would want to offend, so Marvin delayed for some time before he finally found the opportunity to ask in a very polite manner just what had happened to the wheelbarrow.

The twinkly-eyed old Eskimo, proud of his carpentry and likewise his masonry, and always happy to talk about it, explained with enthusiasm, "I use that kind when I make my wall. When I put one rock and mortar, I can push wheelbarrow up fast and give it big hit. That make it sit down tight on other rocks!"

"Kind of hard on my wheelbarrow, don't you think?" Marvin reproved him.

But Kopotuk chose that moment not to understand the English language, and the matter was discussed no further.

Just as the sod igloo at Kalla had been built over a hole in the ground, so was the new log cabin at Shungnak sixty years later. We stooped when we went through the door and walked down two steps to the dirt floor. One small glass window looking over the river took the place of the sealgut skylight; and when all was finished, Kopotuk brought in armfuls of fresh spruce boughs to scatter over the floor for carpeting. Except for his home made stove, there was no furniture in the cabin. He spread his furs on the floor for a bed, stirred up his sourdough hotcakes in a pan on the floor, and ate squatting down with his plate in front of him.

We were lavish in our praises of his new home as was the rest of the village; and for a while after he moved, he had a surplus of visitors. But it wasn't long until he began to complain of arthritis and rheumatism and stiffnesses of all sorts. Marvin had to dig deep into the pill boxes and bottles in the school dispensary to keep him on his feet. Finally Marvin decided to have a talk with him.

"Kopotuk, you've had stiff joints ever since you moved into that new house. If you'd build yourself a low bunk, even a foot or so off the floor and get away from that dampness, I think you would feel better."

Kopotuk was indignant. "I never live in a house with bed and chair and table in my whole life!" he declared. "Too old to start now. I live on floor always. Floor is good for me now."

But then came the business of the bread baking, and that's another story.

A few weeks after the move to the new cabin, Kopotuk called on us. We thought the visit came about because he had given himself a haircut and wanted to show it off. How he managed it we never found out, but it looked as though he had put his soup bowl on like a cap and cut around the edges. His white hair bounced out away from his head like an albino mushroom, and he was proud of his handiwork.

But that wasn't the whole reason for his visit. Once the barbering had been discussed and was out of the way, he came right to the point.

"I eat bread your house some time when I come. Good bread. I think now new house—maybe I cook more. Maybe you teach me how you make bread?"

"Good idea, Charlie!" I agreed. "I think bread good for old man to eat. Keep you young."

"Then you teach me?" he asked eagerly.

"Sure I'll teach you. But I think maybe it's better if you come up to school tomorrow morning and watch the cook make a batch of bread for the school children. It might be easier for you to learn that way."

The next morning at eight o'clock sharp, Kopotuk was at the door for his bread-baking lesson. He didn't need as big a batch as the cook was making; so as she poured and added and mixed and kneaded, he was mentally dividing the ingredients by three and saying out loud, "Three for you, one for Charlie—six for you, two for Charlie." Then, with his recipe crammed into his head, he stopped by my kitchen on the way home.

"You come my house tomorrow when school finish. I have piece of bread for you!"

That afternoon he was back again to talk Marvin out of some choice pieces of packing boxes we had hoarded from supplies that had come in the previous summer. Marvin didn't ask why he needed them, but I soon found out.

When I went down to the village the next day to collect my slice of bread, Kopotuk had three fresh loaves sitting on a wobbly-legged table made from the crating material and covered with a clean white flour sack that had been raveled and spread out flat for a tablecloth. You couldn't, he explained, put a batch of freshly baked home made bread on the floor!

The bread baking created another problem. Like any cook with a new recipe, he was making bread about every

190

other day for a while. But one day he came up to consult with us.

"When I make bread, it have three loaf, but I got only two tin." He held up three and then two fingers to emphasize his point. "So I always use tin from my neighbor. But when Eskimo borrow, he never take tin back empty, so I alla time have to give my neighbor one loaf bread. I think long time about that. Something not right for me. I make three loaf. I only get two loaf."

He had no solution to his problem, but thought maybe we would. So after much thinking it over and exploring all possible avenues of escape, Marvin arrived at an excellent idea.

"Maybe Lou can teach you how to make a smaller batch of dough and you can get it all in your own two tins."

So for the rest of the winter, Kopotuk turned out a two-loaf batch of bread, kept one loaf to eat fresh, and carefully stashed the other loaf on top of his roof to freeze.

Although the table stayed in the house, the bunk-bed never materialized. Kopotuk slept on the floor, fought the rheumatism all winter, and when the rest of the village got hit with the flu, so did he. By the end of the second day we had almost no kids left in school. So we closed the classroom doors and Marvin made the rounds of the village every day with pockets full of pill bottles. Eskimos love to take pills, so he was a welcome visitor; and handfuls of pink and white and brown pills were left behind at every cabin. Every cabin that is, except Kopotuk's. He had his own remedy for flu. He drank three fingers of seal oil from a gallon jug every morning and rubbed kerosene on his chest at night.

Almost any time of day during the cold winter months, we could see people going for firewood or bringing it home. The families with dog teams brought it in by the sledload. Those without dogs either pulled sleds by hand or hauled it on their shoulders or in their arms. Only once did we see anyone manage the firewood problem differently. The native lay reader and his family, temporary residents at Shungnak one year, came back down river from their fishing camp that summer with their sleds, dogs, and household goods loaded on top of a huge raft they had built of freshly cut logs. Once the raft had served its purpose, they tore it apart and had their winter's wood supply.

Even Kopotuk, with all his foresight and ambition, never had more than a few days' supply in storage. So one cold day when he came in after dark with his three dogs pulling a sledload of logs, Marvin asked him, "Why don't you plan ahead and have all this wood cut before winter sets in?"

With a look of tolerant patience, Kopotuk explained.

"I try that once," he said. "All summer I cut and pile wood and have enough for whole winter. Then old lady get sick. She got no wood. I got wood, so I give her some. Then young girl have baby bad sick. She can't leave baby. She can't get wood. I have to give her wood. Then we have long cold many days. Many mans can't go for wood. Many houses cold. I still got wood. I give more wood to peoples. Pretty soon I got no wood too, so I never bring in plenty wood again, I go every day just like other peoples."

Once during a visit, Kopotuk made reference to his daughters. We both registered some surprise, I'm sure, because somehow we had never thought of our old friend as being a family man. It was many months later when we knew him much better, that he offered more information on his personal life. It seems that as a young man he had married and had two daughters. Then a white man coming into the area met his wife, and she eventually took the girls and went away with him. It must have been a blow to Kopotuk, because as he told us the story his eyes filled with tears.

Some months later he received an official sounding letter from Nome saying that his wife was suing for divorce and the hearing would come before the court on a specified date the following mid-winter. Kopotuk assumed the letter was a summons for him to appear in court on that date. So that fall as soon as the rivers froze and winter set in, he harnessed his dogs, filled his sled with supplies, and started out on the long trip of several hundred miles to Nome. He had been to Kotzebue many times, but knew nothing of the area between the Kobuk Valley and Nome on the underside of the Seward Peninsula. He followed his nose and the advice of the villagers he met along the way, and arrived in Nome on schedule, only to discover that his presence hadn't even been requested. So he took on a new load of supplies, turned his team around, and started the long lonesome trek back to the land that was home and that he knew. Early the next spring he finally mushed into Shungnak again.

When the girls grew up and married, they came back to Shungnak to visit their father; and although they never visited the years we lived there, they always kept in touch with him.

One morning during our last year in the village, Kopotuk came to the office to have me write a letter for him. I had written letters for him before, so I knew the procedure. I always sat at the typewriter and waited dutifully as he clasped his hands behind his back, looked down at the floor, and paced thoughtfully back and forth while he dictated like an executive, and I typed like a secretary. Then, because I was a terrible typist, I'd have to redo the whole letter, throw the original copy into the waste basket, and submit the second one to him for his signature. But I wasn't expecting what he had in mind on this particular day when he came to see us.

He had just received word that his youngest daughter was in the Native Service hospital at Kotzebue dying of tuberculosis. He clasped his hands behind his back, lowered his head, began his slow pacing, and dictated the most eloquent message I have ever heard. It began, "My dear daughter Otha: The time has come for you to meet your Maker. I want you to go without fear, because you have led a good and Christian life."

What he said beyond that I don't recall, but the letter was short—just one page long—and it ended with the words, "Your father, Charlie Coffin." I carefully recopied the message in longhand on a sheet of paper, let him sign it, and sealed it in an envelope for him.

Long after he left the office, I sat reading and rereading

the original copy. It was beautiful—the most straight-from-the-heart piece of literature I had ever seen. More than anything in the world, I wanted to tuck it away in my notebook to take back home with me and some day read to my grandchildren, or to a literature class I might be teaching. But somehow it seemed too much like prying into a private life I had no business with, so I tore it to bits and threw it in the waste basket.

Both Kopotuk and Otha are now gone, and I have wished many times since that I could peek into the notebook and find the letter I destroyed.

CHAPTER XX

A LOSS AND A GAIN

I've never believed that growing up is a steady, unbroken process. It comes in spurts. Successes, failures, happiness, heartbreaks, and tragedies—those are the things that make men and women out of us.

I did my first real growing up the year I was twelve. For long months I lay flat on my back in the grip of rheumatic fever, and it gave me a lot of time to think about what I wanted out of life. I already realized I couldn't have everything; but I vowed I would some day walk again and from there on I would pick and choose and take only the best of what life had to offer.

I made another long step toward maturity in the depth of the Great Depression when Dad lost the farm he had built from the ground up and lived on for 20 years. I was 16 when we had to pack up our personal belongings and walk away from everything that had been home to us. There was a lot of bitterness in our hearts, but out of that bitterness grew strength enough to start all over again.

I faced another of those growing up periods in late October of 1946. The river was freezing and transportation at a standstill. While the floe ice was growing and gathering into masses that floated downstream until they finally reached from shore to shore, we were isolated. Neither boat nor dog team could use the river, and even airplanes had no place to land. The villagers who had been out at their fish camps all summer had to come back early enough to travel by boat or wait until November when the ice was solid enough for dogsleds. It ended up about fifty fifty. We had half the people on hand before freezeup, and that gave us just enough children to warrant opening school, but not enough to start any real schoolwork. We did as much of our extra-curricular work those three weeks as possible. This involved taking the children down river in the big boat to pick cranberries for our hot lunches, decorating the classrooms for the late fall season, or bringing up a supply of water from the river. We had had some trouble with the rails that brought the hoist car up hill, so the water didn't get hauled on Friday as we had planned. Instead, the school boys, Robert, and Marvin spent their day repairing the track. The older boys loved this hoist car operation, so decided they would come back Saturday morning to haul water.

Saturday proved to be a miserable day—cold, overcast, and with high, blustery winds that carried the taste of snow. Marvin and the boys were hauling their water all right, but with winter parkas and mitts on, and their ruffs drawn up over their heads against the sharp wind.

We thought our ears were playing tricks on us when we heard the steady swelling and fading of an airplane motor from up river. A pilot would have to be out of his mind to be up in this stuff. But a plane it was—a little black two-place L-5 bobbing and rolling erratically through the turbulance and overcast from the CAA station to the village.

"Mr. Collins! It Mr. Collins!" shouted one of the boys.

"It sure is," agreed Marvin in amazement. "What on earth is he doing in the air on a day like this?"

Dick made a couple of bumpy passes above us before

he was finally able to dip a wing over the schoolhouse and drop out a roll of toilet paper. This was standard practice with pilots who wanted to deliver a message or a parcel from the air. The message was fastened to the loose end of the roll, the paper unrolled like a long kite tail as it fell to the ground, and led the way to the spot where it landed.

In our case, it didn't work. The roll had hardly left the plane when a blast of wind ripped it in two. The message went one way and the roll of paper the other. But we could see them both sailing off in the general direction of the tundra behind the school. Everyone raced to the top of the hill and fanned out across the grass hummocks in search of the note.

One of the boys finally located it and came running to Marvin. The message was to us, so he opened it and pulled out a piece of yellow paper—the kind telegrams are typed on. He scanned it quickly, and I knew from the sudden shock on his face that it wasn't good news. I reached to take it from him, but he pulled it away. The whole village was in a circle around us; and he said, "Wait. Let's go into the house first."

But I wouldn't wait. I reached again, and this time he let me have it. The message was from my brother Troy back in Wisconsin and had been sent only a few hours earlier. Our mother had died that morning.

I did my crying, but quietly. When Marvin tried to console me, I told him not to feel sorry for me because it would only make me worse; and he complied. Instead, he praised me for pulling myself together and putting a supper on the table that evening.

Although Marvin told me I could go home if I wished, we both knew I couldn't. This thing had happened at the worst time of the year, and no way could I get out of Shungnak. More than that, the last barge of the season had already gone down the river and no mail plane arrived for a long, long time. It was almost Christmas before I could send a letter to my family to let them know I had received the message.

* * *

Back in his days at Elim, Marvin didn't have a transmitter at his station, but had ready access to the facilities at the army base at Moses Point. He assumed when we went to Shungnak that since we were with the federal government we could send and receive messages through the CAA. It was quite a setback when he found out this was not the case. The CAA had established some rigid rules, and would carry no messages other than its own, except for real emergencies. Mother's death had been called an emergency, but few other messages were.

As the weeks dragged on and no mail plane arrived to carry a letter back to my family, Marvin vowed we would never be caught in a situation like this again. Upstairs in one of our many little storage rooms, was an old transmitter, long outdated and completely on strike. Marvin had looked it over a few times, but had always walked away with a sigh and a shrug of his shoulders. He considered it a lost cause.

Now we had a real need for a means of communication. He carried it downstairs and completely dismembered it.

"Do you know that much about transmitters?" I questioned.

"Well—it's no good the way it is. I may as well experiment with it."

For weeks the transmitter was strung all over our living room floor and I began to wonder if I would ever be able to vacuum the rug again. It got a little embarrassing when travelling personel came through and had to be entertained at the dining room table because there was no place to sit in the living room—especially when most of our guests were of the opinion that the transmitter would never be in one piece again.

They were wrong. Toward spring the pieces little by little fell into place, and the time came when we could turn the knobs and get a carrier. Eventually we were on the air with our own call letters and regular daily schedules with the ACS (Alaska Communications System) and the Native Service hospital in Kotzebue.

The transmitter opened up a whole new world for the entire village. When someone was sick, we could describe his symptoms to the doctor in Kotzebue and get his advice. If the mail pilot was making plans to start up river the next day, we knew it. And messages concerning school or village matters from our office in Juneau came through by wire in a matter of hours. If someone in the village had an urgent message to send to a friend or relative in another village, we could make arrangements with the teacher from that village a day ahead of time to have both parties on hand at the same time for their transmission. They loved to talk over the radio.

Several families had their own little receivers, and never missed the afternoon schedules. Sometimes a youngster would come to school in the morining, slip up to my desk, and say, "I hear Mr. Warbelow on radio last night!" Or Robert would comment when he came to work in the morning, "Look like boat got in Kotzebue with freight last night, I hear."

Those little transmitters in the villages were the best morale builders a teacher could have. Every evening after the doctor was off the air and the ACS telegrams had all been transmitted, the airways became a regular old-fashioned party line. The teachers stayed on the air for the rest of the evening. Usually two carried on a conversation while all the others listened in; but sometimes a third party or even a fourth would have to cut in and give an opinion on anything from what to do about a broken down light plant to whose sourdough starter was the liveliest.

Carl Johnson whose wife was the teacher in a small village was our most entertaining participant in these evening exchanges.

"My wife says I embarrass her when I get on this radio because I don't talk good English, but you know I ain't never had much book learnin'."

A few days later he was lamenting the fact that he had tried to mix up some cement with his wife's Mixmaster and ruined the whole machine. But his biggest blunder came the night he let it be known all over the Arctic that he had shot a moose out of season; and the next day a game warden flew in from Kotzebue to confiscate his meat and fine him fifty dollars.

Periodically we would all receive officious letters from whoever it was that controlled the airways telling us this round robin stuff must come to an end and the transmissions be limited to business only. So for a month or two there would be complete silence after the schedules from Kotzebue. Then little by little a few of the braver ones eased back on the air with short messages to neighbors. In no time at all every teacher in the Arctic was right there at his transmitter again and the gossip flowed until the voice of authority cut them off again.

CHAPTER XXI

THE CO-OP STORE

Our second winter at Shungnak started out much the same as the first. As days darkened and temperatures plummeted, cabin fever and irritabilities began to dominate the village. Early in the winter Jonas Bale had lost his outboard motor in a poker game, but then refused to give it up. This was the ultimate in poor sportsmanship, so the village ostracized him. When the pressure got to the point where he couldn't face it any more, he hooked up his dogs, left the village, and didn't come back until after the Christmas holidays. While he was gone, the Council took the opportunity to vote him out of the vice-presidency.

Another flare-up of tempers came when most of the people began to gather at Violet Perry's house every evening to dance. One of the elder Council members renounced the dancing as being not only unchristian, but illegal according to Council rules. The dancing continued, and finally he came up to school in a fury one day to announce that he was resigning from the board. I'm sure he thought this drastic act would bring the village to its senses and people would beg him to take back his office. But not so. The Council held a meeting and elected one of their best dancers to replace him. At the same time they struck from their village code any law banning dances that might have existed; and legalized Eskimo dancing became a fact.

These little revolts were never permanent things. At the next Council meeting the elder was discretely reinstated to his position on the board, and he accepted the office without comment.

Food was in short supply. The hot lunches eased the pressure, because they took care of one meal a day for the children and the cooks. But the trips to Kobuk to buy groceries weren't fun during the winter, and prices were high. Self-pity and boredom were elbowing their way into every cabin.

"Boredom is a dangerous thing," Marvin told one of his classes one day. "There isn't enough activity going on here this winter to keep people interested. You younger generation should be thinking about that. By the time you're old enough to be running the village affairs, you should have something figured out to keep everyone busy."

So began the talk of a native store at Shungnak. Kobuk was ten miles up river. For some of the widows and old women, or unmarried girls with children, it was a real hardship to get groceries. We had seen them in the summer time poling boats along the bank on an all-day trip to Kobuk, and in the winter time packing sacks of flour home on their backs or pulling loaded handsleds. This wasn't so bad during the summer months or even in late spring and early fall when the river was frozen. But in the dead of winter it meant walking most of the trip in the dark and facing bitter cold winds. Ray Chaplain who was a good trader, and his wife did their best to make the trip easier for their Shungnak customers. They always had a warm fire and a pot of coffee or tea waiting for them. But even that didn't shorten the trip between the two villages.

We did a lot of talking in the village that winter, with the pros and cons of a native store being tossed around from one meeting to the next. We needed a post office too, so the post office project grew right along with the store.

There were those in the village like the Tories of Revolution days who didn't want to upset the apple cart. Chaplain had served them well and they were averse to angering Harry. But we had the others who liked the idea of being able to walk to the end of the village for a box of soda.

Marvin's sales pitch was evident everywhere—at Council meetings, village meetings, and at every gathering on the foot path or around a dog food fire.

"Look, fellows," I'd hear him say, "you can't just remain static. Sure, you've gone to Kobuk for years to get your grub, but don't you ever want to better yourselves? Your grandfathers were satisfied to pole up river all the way from Kotzebue, but do you do it? No! You want outboard motors. They lived without salt and canned peaches and radios. But are you willing to do it? No! So why go on making these long trips to Kobuk when we could have a store right here in Shungnak? Did you ever think about the fact that the supplies for the store at Kobuk go right by your front door on the barge every fall and then you have to go ten miles up river to bring them back? If the barge can take supplies to Kobuk, it can bring supplies to Shungnak."

"But what about Ray?" someone asked. "Ray live here long time. He make living that store. He need us."

"In the long run, it isn't going to hurt Ray," Marvin argued. "These villages are going to grow. With more nurses and doctors and medicine, we don't have so many people die. More babies live, so the Eskimo population is growing. Then we're going to have white people moving into the country again just like those old prospectors did fifty years ago. Only this time they'll stay. They'll open up mines here because you have minerals. Ray's store will have plenty of business. You'll need two stores!"

Little by little the credibility gap closed, but no matter how much everyone talked, they always ended up facing one unsolved problem—finances. The Alaska Native Service gave us the boost we needed.

Native stores hadn't as yet existed in Alaska, but our Juneau office was just about to get some financing to create a revolving fund that could be used to build stores in the villages. As a store was established and making money, it would pay back its original loan that could then be used to finance another store somewhere else. Money wasn't easy to come by in those days, though. If we wanted the loan, we had to prove our worth. In short, we had to put up our own building, raise money to finance our initial stock of groceries, and operate for a year before we would be eligible for the ten thousand dollars we wanted to borrow.

The majority of the village was finally convinced that we'd build our store. But where was the money coming from? Our only possible means was to convince the villagers they should pledge some or all of their muskrat skins that spring for groceries they would be getting the next fall. But Eskimos don't think that way. This was a way of life they didn't like. They could take their skins to Kobuk as soon as they were off the stretching boards, and bring home groceries and guns and bright calico; and that was what they had done all their lives. So it took a lot of salesmanship to get us over the next hurdle. And of course there was always lurking in the back of everyone's mind the fear that the teachers might fail them. If we made the great effort and then the store never materialized, those who had taken a stand in favor of it would be in a bad way. How would they ever face up to the people at Kobuk again?

By mid-March, most of the families with boats and proper gear had moved out to their muskrat camps. So as soon as break-up cleared the river of ice, Marvin and Flip and I spent our days in the boat visiting every family rat camp up and down the river and to the ends of every tributary. We needed muskrats badly. I'm sure each family had made up its mind before we arrived as to what extent it would support the store. Some had all their skins bundled up and ready for us to take back to the village for safekeeping. Others split their catch down the middle. They'd send one bundle back home and keep the other

204

in reserve for the store at Kobuk. By this time, the idea of the store had been fairly well accepted, so there weren't more than two or three families who refused to have any part in it at all.

Next we had to have a building we could call our store. In this case, Lady Luck had been sitting on our side of the fence. During the depression days of the early thirties, the village had started to build a good sized log building under the CCC program. Marvin asked Jonas Smith about it one day.

"They call it Happy House," he told us, "and it suppose to be recreation hall. But I think that Happy House have a plenty unhappy end. Before we ever get it built, that roof fall in and we never finish."

Marvin had been listening intently. "Why would the roof collapse?" he asked.

Jonas shrugged his shoulders. "We think poor engineering. That foreman don't know how to build a roof everybody say."

The village had passed it off as a big joke. So there sat the Happy House, waiting for a rebirth.

We didn't ask any questions or get permission from anyone. We just decided we'd appropriate what was left of the CCC project and put the logs to work. Rat season ended June 7 and the real fishing season didn't start until July, so we planned to build our store the second week in June.

CHAPTER XXII

BUILDING OF THE STORE

With the end of muskrat season, people packed their tents and cooking equipment, loaded families and dogs into their boats, and moved back into the village. From forty miles up and down river they came, and our store-building project began. During the day the men worked with the logs while the women cooked food to keep them going. Daniel Stringer was not only village chief, but a knowledgeable cabin builder; so he was in charge of the work force. This had been a trying time and a difficult decision for Daniel. He was one of Chaplain's closest friends and supporters, and had for several years been the pilot on Ray's boat when it went to Kotzebue for supplies every summer. Although his heart was at Kobuk, his better judgment told him he had no choice but to take charge of the building project. Enthusiasm was high at the moment and it was evident that if he didn't take the reins in hand at this time, one of the younger men in the village would. That he couldn't let happen. But his

207

strained relations with the people at Kobuk caused him much concern.

Marvin worked with the crew all day long, while I made cold coke drinks and hot coffee to keep up everyone's morale.

The Happy House logs got some close scrutiny. "Some of these logs pretty rotten some places," Daniel noted, and wrinkled his brows. "Don't know about them." "But we don't need a store as big as the Happy House, do we?" asked Marvin. "The bigger the store, the more wood to heat it."

"That right," agreed one of the younger fellows. "If we make cabin smaller, we can cut off bad ends of logs and use just best part."

"Sure," chimed in another. "I pretty lazy anyway. Don't like to lift big logs!"

This remark, he knew, would bring a chorus of laughter, which it did. And the dimensions of the new store were thus established.

Every evening after work hours, we played games or had boat and kayak races. Sometimes we opened the classrooms and suffered through one of those wild brawls they called a basketball game. Marvin and I didn't like it, but we were determined to keep the village together long enough to finish that building.

What we thought was going to be a three-day project lasted more than two weeks. At the end of the first week, the men decided they would stay over until Monday and work a second week. Sunday was church day and dress up day and there was no thought of store building. By Monday our crew had dwindled. Some of the fellows who didn't really have their hearts in the job right from the beginning used the week-end to move out of the village again; so by Monday we were down to a hard core crew of a half dozen men. It was an education for us just to see those people plan and work together Eskimo style. They spent hours hewing logs, fitting corners, and then going into a conference about whether it was right or not. Every day Marvin took a boatload of kids up river to gather moss for chinking between the logs.

By the end of our second week, the crew had dwindled even further. Chief Daniel grew quiet and withdrawn. He began coming to work late and quitting early. Finally the day came when he didn't appear at all. But it was imperative that we get our building closed in, so Marvin kept driving. With the roof finished, two windows and a homemade door installed, and part of the floor covered with whipsawed lumber, we called it quits. The rest of the floor could come later.

We had promised a potlatch when the store was finished, and potlatch we did. Marvin bought twelve pounds of reindeer meat from the herder. I made four big kettles of reindeer stew thickened with rice, and a double batch of brown bread. Because the women in the village were much better coffee makers than I was, I took my can of coffee down to them.

"If you want to add anything else to our potlatch, you're welcome to do it," I suggested.

"Maybe we can make some doughnut," Irene offered.

There was a minute or so of confering in Eskimo and then Irene addressed me again. "Yes, they say. We can fix."

They cooked up a big wooden platter of salmon trout, made some fried doughnuts Eskimo style without any holes in them, and a heaping pan of ah-koo-tuk.

Ah-koo-tuk is Eskimo ice cream. To make it was a day-long job, and only a few women specialized in it. Minnie Jack, Robert Cleveland's daughter, was one of them. She started out with blobs of raw reindeer or caribou tallow in a big dishpan. Working it with both hands, she squeezed and kneaded until it softened, then folded in some seal oil and whipped it in a circular motion until it became a pile of froth heaped up like whipped cream in the pan. Then came the finishing touches. She folded in some sugar and added berries or pieces of dried fish. The berries were either blueberries or lingenberries (the Norweigen cranberry), and sometimes she used raisins. My favorite version of ah-koo-tuk had both raisins and lingenberries in it. The berries cut the greasy taste and the raisins added more sweetening. Minnie had gone all out for this great occasion, and our ice cream was speckled with blue and red.

Considering the fact that our crew had shrunk to almost nothing those last few days, there was an amazing turnout at the potlatch. We spread the food out on the ground in front of Robert's cabin near the store, and sat cross-legged in a big circle to eat, each of us with his own tin dish. I sat between Minnie, all rosy-cheeked and radiant with the success of her ice cream, and elderly Sarah Cummings who was a bit of a village gossip and inclined to let the fringes of her envy show. Everyone had high praises for my stew and bread.

"Sure think I get fat on good bread like that!"

"Maybe we all better go back to school. Kids say they have good bread like this every day."

"We have reindeer stew this way some time too," chimed in one of the youngsters.

We all agreed that the salmon was perfect; and the doughnuts disappeared with many a remark about how the women should make them more often. But the loudest praises of all came for the ah-koo-tuk that is a super special thing with the village.

"I never have ah-koo-tuk since one year ago!"

"Minnie makes the best Eskimo ice cream I ever ate!" I declared emphatically.

With all these lavish compliments, Minnie's cheeks grew rosier.

Those of us who had brought dishes and spoons ate our ice cream in proper manner, but the others—mostly youngsters who didn't rate a place at the table, but hovered around in an outer circle and snatched whatever they could—scooped up gobs of the ice cream with their hands. Sarah, avoiding the ah-koo-tuk and turning a deaf ear to the situation as long as she could, finally tasted it. Then, leaning toward me, she carefully cupped her hand between her mouth and my ear and whispered, "Little too much seal oil!"

* * *

Once the store became a reality, the project was more convincing, and people who had invested only a few skins began stopping by to leave more. Even some of the total sceptics decided it might be a good idea to have a couple dozen ratskins pledged, just to keep a foot in the door. If the store survived, they could have the fun of being part of it; and if it went over the brink, they could go back to Kobuk.

Rats were bringing in the vicinity of a dollar apiece in those days, and we estimated that our total collection wouldn't go over two thousand dollars. This meant confining our order of supplies to the bare essentials. No calico, no candy, and no guns or knives or outboard motors. Our list consisted mainly of flour, sugar, tea, coffee, salt, soda, canned milk, and brown soap. Mark Cleveland had a sturdy inboard motor cabin boat, so he made the trip to Kotzebue for our load of supplies. Marvin had already made arrangements with Louie Rotman who had one of the main trading posts in Kotzebue, to buy our skins and supply our groceries.

The day came when we heard that steady chug-chug of a motor boat rounding the last bend into sight of the village.

"Mark come! Mark come!" called out one lone voice, and the whole village took up the chorus.

"Mark come!"

"Boat here! Boat here for store!"

"Ya-a! Ya-a-a-a!"

All of us were dancing up and down as though we had an army of victorious soldiers returning to the homeland.

Lightering was always fun when Archie's barge with our school supplies came in every fall, but in no way could it compare with lightering our own supplies off one of the village boats and stacking boxes and sacks in our own store. No one was on the payroll, but nobody cared. With only a third of our building boasting a floor, we had to stack everything in one end. But that didn't matter either. The hundred pound sacks of flour were big enough

211

to be laid across the floor joists and more sacks stacked on top of them.

When it was all finished, we sat on big rounds of fire wood or floor joists in the unfinished part of the store, reminisced about our big venture from the very beginning, and built air castles about what we had ahead of us.

Most of those air castles came to pass. We did get our floor finished and we did get our post office. So we partitioned off a little room in one corner of the store for the post office, and set up an oil drum stove by the door. Marvin ran a long extension cord down the hill from the school and hung one light bulb from the ceiling. That was the frosting on the cake; it was the only electric light in the village.

Choosing a storekeeper was an occasion that warranted a meeting of the entire village. The harsh feelings that had split the village in the early stages of the store project had worn their edges off, and we now had a general feeling of acceptance. Our turnout at the meeting represented most of the village.

Marvin, in charge of the gathering, came right to the point. Who did we want for storekeeper?

There was a long silence, and finally the room began to buzz with short, and then longer exchanges in Eskimo. Marvin and interpreter Charlie Sheldon stood by patiently waiting for some decision to come forth. A statement was finally addressed to Charlie and he translated into English.

"The people say Daniel Stringer is our chief. They think he should be storekeeper."

Daniel flushed with pride, and his tight lips twitched, but he made no comment.

There were two other names written on the blackboard beneath Daniel's, but this was only a token gesture. Chief Stringer was chosen, almost unanimously, to be our first storekeeper. He felt it was time to make a statement, so stood up and accepted his new position.

"This time important to us all. We need store in Shungnak. We all work hard to make it. We still help store for Ray Chaplain too because our store small yet.

Many things we don't have. We thank Mr. Warbelow now for how he help to get our store built. He says our store will grow big. Maybe we see that some day!"

I was the first postmaster, but I didn't like the bookwork. We knew our time in Shungnak was limited, so that gave me a good excuse to start training a new postmaster. There again we had to use the trial and error method before we discovered that George Cleveland took to it like a duck to water, and he never gave up the position.

We heard from George over the next few years as we moved about the Arctic from one village to another. He was a good letter writer, as were any of the Eskimos we ever corresponded with. I still have one of his letters:

Shungnak, Alaska
January 16, 1952

Dear Mr. and Mrs. Warbelow;

Since I haven't write for long time, so I thought I'd better write a letter, and tell you some news about the post office here in our village. It's getting along fairly well now, they have raise my salary effective July first up to $685.44 that of course plus 25% differential on top, that's sure look good to me. So for that matter I would like to say many thanks once more for learning me how to run that job, which I would never learn without your help. I'm still having lots of difficult but not bad as first start. Every time when I got my Quarterly Reports all ready to send in, heres the words I'd always say, Once again it's time for me to say thanks to Gen. Supt. Don C. Foster who send Mr. and Mrs. Warbelow up here to be our teachers, and teach me how to run this job.

I'm having a hard time to learn my new typewriter, takes me pretty close to two hours to write this letters.

All the peoples are in good condition on their health but they all run pretty short on food, they didn't get much fish last summer, because of high water all summer. But lots of ptarmigans womens sure like to put their snares out but the weather is not suitable to do anything like that, sure been stormy after Christmas.

213

That is all I can think of at the present time, regard to your family.

> Very Sincerely yours,
> George O. Cleveland and
> family

Just to set the record straight, I'd like to explain that the salary of $685.44 George quoted wasn't for one month. It represented his earning for a year's work.

* * *

The store created a natural meeting place, so organizations began to blossom. Among them was the Jade Club. We elected officers, set a price on raw jade of two dollars a pound, and agreed that any sales would become common property of the club.

We got it organized just in time too. Shortly after that two men from a Chicago newspaper arrived via mail plane to get a story on the Shungnak jade. The club members came up to school to meet them and be interviewed. That night Marvin and our guests sat up into the wee hours visiting.

When Marvin finally came to bed, he whispered, "These fellows are as interested in getting some jade for themselves as they are in getting a story for the newspaper. I'd better go down to the village first thing in the morning to be sure all the club members are on hand with all the company jade."

But when Marvin got up, our two men were already in the living room waiting for him. He had no opportunity to leave the house. So as soon as I had the coffee pot on the stove, I slipped out the back door and down the hill through the brush to the store. A few of our jade club members were already there in anticipation of early morning customers.

"Marvin says to tell you these visitors are interested in buying jade. Can you have it all here in the store when they come down?"

"We figure that way," came a mischievous voice from the circle around the stove. "We already vote, and price of jade just come up to two dollar fifty a pound!"

214

With winks and smiles and nods of heads, they all agreed in unison, "Okay!"

Price didn't stop our two visitors. Down in the store after breakfast, they picked themselves some nice pieces of jade. One of them chose a forty-pound rock and paid for it with one hundred silver dollars he was carrying in a red stocking cap. The jade club had made its first big sale.

CHAPTER XXIII

KEWALIK

Freeze-up, in mid-October, was always a depressing time in the Arctic. The river was our highway. It served as our waterway during the summer months; and in the winter became a landing strip for planes and a highway for dog teams and snowshoers. But for three weeks or so during October, while the chunks of floe ice were too thick for boats to navigate and not solid enough for dog teams, we were completely isolated. Our mail came up from Kotzebue on Archie Ferguson's barge once a month during June, July, August, and September, and by plane the rest of the year. But from September until November when the ice had firmed up, we were at the mercy of the weather and the pilots, and usually went that whole two months with no word from the Outside.

For days we watched the freeze-up process slowly but surely taking place. As September slipped away and the sun dropped lower and temperatures tumbled, the river water began to drop and slow its pace. Then on chilly mornings we saw small, thin sheets of ice forming, break-

217

ing from the shore, and crumbling into smaller pieces as they were caught up in the current. With each day, the ice formations became thicker and stronger; and finally they no longer broke into pieces, but zigzagged and twisted through eddies into the mainstream where they were joined by others like them, and started the long ride toward Kotzebue. As the water level dropped steadily and the chunks of floe increased in size and number, we began to see the evidence of small ice jams. If enough ice piled up shoulder to shoulder to form an irregular but solid fence across the river, nothing moved. The loose ice from upstream was imprisoned behind the fence and hung there struggling for an opening to break through. These jams at first didn't last very long, because with the constant bobbing up and down on the flowing water under them, all it took was for one block of ice to shift sideways and break through, and the whole jam disintegrated and moved out.

While all this was going on, the shelf ice was steadily freezing out further and further into the river. Since it was anchored firmly to the shore, and as the water became more shallow and ice found another firm hold on the river bottom, it didn't move out with the rest of the mass. Shelf ice stretching out from each bank of the river further every day was constantly narrowing the channel between them.

Then one morning the mail plane roared in from down river way, buzzed the village once, and went on to the CAA field to land.

The village came to life in a hurry, and with moans and groans we watched the plane make a big circle and disappear below the tree tops three miles up river.

"No way to get that mail down here now!" lamented Daniel.

"Three week almost before we can get dog team on that ice," agreed Jonas.

Marvin had built a little sixteen foot speed boat from half inch plywood the summer before to replace the cumbersome *Flip Eye*. This one we had christened *Kay*.

"Of course, there's always the *Kay*," Marvin ventured.

But the *Kay* and all the other boats in the village had been dragged up on shore, turned upside down to keep them dry inside, and were anchored for the winter. Marvin should probably have given a thought to his experience with ice our first spring at Shungnak; but if he did, it was outweighed by thoughts of that mailpouch sitting up at Dick's house.

"If you fellowswill help me get that boat into the river, I'll go get the mail! There's plenty of open water in the middle of the Kobuk yet."

Everyone was quick to agree with him. After all, they weren't the ones making the trip!

Up the hill he went to get his outboard motor from the basement while the rest of the men hauled the *Kay* a few feet out onto the shelf ice and fastened the motor in place. Marvin crawled into the boat and held the motor up while a half dozen fellows pushed it out to the edge of the ice and it plopped into the water like a muskrat diving off shore.

"Kewalik!" someone shouted, and that was Marvin's Eskimo name from that moment on. In Eskimo, Kewalik means muskrat.

He gave a couple of quick yanks on the pull rope and started the motor before the current had time to head it downstream; and with a real hero's sendoff and cheers from one end of the village to the other, he nosed into the oncoming ice and made his crooked way to the middle of the river, dodging ice cakes. We all waited on the bank until he rounded the first bend of the river, and then went back to our separate safe little homes to wait for his return.

By the time Flip and I got back up the hill, it was nearly noon. Before three o'clock it would be dark; but with good luck, Marvin should be home by that time. I think I had an uneasy feeling from the very beginning that it wasn't going to happen, and it didn't. Within fifteen minutes, that house was beginning to look awfully big and lonesome for just one little cocker spaniel and me. I stood at first one window and then another and watched the river with its fast-thickening ice chunks, and the grey sky darkening at an alarming pace. Flip stayed at my side and whimpered a bit now and then and nudged my leg with his wet nose to remind me that he was still there.

I made a trip or two back down to the village where a few people were still wandering around outside, and our alarm grew fast when two fellows came walking up from down river carrying their kayaks on their shoulders and said the river ice had formed a solid jam just down below. That meant that the ice in the village and on up river would soon be jamming, and no way could a boat get through.

By four o'clock night had settled in and I was close to panic. Mark Cleveland came up the hill to start my light plant.

"Anything I can do for you, Lou?" he asked as he hesitated at the kitchen door.

But there wasn't, and he knew it; and after an awkward silence, he left. White women are always a mystery to the native people, and they don't know what sort of reactions to expect from us. I wanted to cry, but there were no tears.

I began to think about the two-way radio Marvin had put together. I had never learned how to operate it. Marvin and the Collinses had talked on various occasions, and at least I knew how to transmit to them, but I had no idea how to tune them in to receive.

They had a floodlight on a tall pole outside their building, and in the dark I could see the light. It gave me a sudden inspiration.

I turned the transmitter on and began to call in the blind.

"Calling CAA. Calling CAA. This is Lou Warbelow calling Shungnak CAA! I don't know your call letters and I don't know how to tune you in so I can receive. But if you hear me, will you turn your flood light off and on once. Wait until I have time to get to the bedroom window so I can see it."

I had plenty of time because they had to go downstairs and outdoors to switch the light.

Sure enough, the light went off and on again! My spirits

boomed and I had a shiver of excitement when I saw it. So back at my transmitter I told them my predicament.

"I don't know how to tune you in, but I'll ask you some questions you can answer by yes or no. Will you flip your light once for yes and twice for no. Marvin started up to your place for the mail before noon and hasn't come home yet."

It was a slow operation, but it worked. Little by little I learned that Marvin had arrived at the station and started home. But beyond that, I couldn't find out much. I was puzzled by the fact that he hadn't even made it up there until almost three o'clock; and they obviously were trying to tell me something more, but had no way of doing it. So we gave up and I turned my radio off.

It was still only six o'clock and how I was ever going to get through that long night ahead of me I couldn't imagine. Then I thought about the fact that the store had a wood heater in it and the storekeeper always banked the fire at night to keep things from freezing. Maybe I'd feel better if I went down there where I could watch the river a little closer. So I bundled up, assured Flip I would be right back, and started down the hill in the dark.

Just before I reached the store, it occurred to me that the door would be locked; but since I was this far, I'd give it a try just in case it wasn't. Sure enough, the knob turned and the door opened.

I walked in and stood there waiting for my eyes to adjust to the darkness. The only light was a trickle of flame I could see through the front of the stove. There was absolute silence in the room, but after those first few seconds I could begin to see a circle of dark forms on the floor in front of me. Then I realized it was made up of the men in the village, sitting there cross-legged, in conference.

I couldn't fathom the meaning of this strange situation, and no one spoke or moved. Finally, with my heart pounding right up to my throat and my hands shaking inside my mittens, I asked of no one in particular, "What are you men doing here?"

There was another silence, and then someone said,

221

"We're talking about what we should do about Marvin."

That did it. I turned around, and without another word I left the building and stumbled up the hill in the dark as fast as I could go. Flip was waiting at the door for me, so I hugged him and cried into his fur, and paced the floor endlessly for what seemed hours. No one came near me again, and I knew why. I was something they didn't know how to cope with.

Just before ten o'clock there was a sudden pounding on the front door. I ran to open it and there stood Charlie Douglas, our dancing Santa Claus, all out of breath.

Between gasps, he said, "Marvin says to turn switch on so we can have light in the store!"

"Marvin!" I couldn't believe it. "Where is he?"

"He down at the store!" And away he went into the darkness.

Now I was shaking all over again. I flipped the switch for the long extension cord Marvin had strung down the hill, grabbed my parka, and was right behind Charlie by the time he got to the bottom.

The store was full of excited people, and Marvin was squatted in the middle of the floor dumping out a whole big sackful of mail, handing it out piece by piece as he read names. There was laughing and joking and everyone wanting to know what had happened to him. He was getting as big a hero's return as he had a hero's departure ten hours earlier, and enjoying it to the utmost.

When the mail had been distributed, he said, "Now if you'll all sit down, I'll tell you what happens to a guy who's dumb enough to get caught in the river at freeze-up time."

I picked a spot as close to Marvin as I could, and we all settled in to listen.

"Everything went fine until I was about a mile from the CAA. Then those ice cakes splashing up against the boat evidently threw cold water into the carburator and my motor stalled. There was still enough open water to maneuver it, so I used a paddle and got the boat to shore. I pulled it up on dry land and walked the rest of the way."

"That's why you didn't get up there until three o'clock!" I interrupted.

"How did you know what time I got there?" he wanted to know.

"Oh, I'll tell you later. Just go on."

He gave me a puzzled look, but could see he wasn't going to get any more information, so went on with his story.

"Dick wanted me to stay there, but I didn't want to waste any time, so I put that mail pouch over my shoulder and walked back to the boat. The motor was useless, but I figured I could float back home. I knew that eventually I'd have to cross the river, and the boat was the only way I could do it.

"Well, I was out in the water and halfway home when I could see that the ice in front of me wasn't moving, and there was no way to get through. So I got that paddle working again and began to juggle ice cakes back and forth so I could work through them to this side of the river. For a while I thought I wasn't going to make it, but I did. So I pulled the boat up on shore and turned it upside down with the motor under it. There it sits right now."

"Did you drain the water out of the motor?" asked Robert.

"You bet I did! I was lucky it hadn't already frozen. I put that lousy mail sack on my back again and walked home along the river bank. I'll tell you, I could have used a good flashlight. Those willows are bad enough to get through in daylight, but in the dark—wow!

"But I had my little bit of fun anyway." Here he stopped long enough to give Charlie Douglas a wink. Charlie blushed and squirmed, and they both laughed.

"I had to cross this slough down here at the end of the village by Douglas's house. I didn't think the ice would be strong enough to hold me, so I got down on my hands and knees and crawled across it real easy like, and kept shoving the mail pouch as far ahead of me as I could so I wouldn't have all the weight in one place. Well, I was just a little over halfway across when poor old Charlie

223

here comes out of his mother's house and sees me. I suppose I looked like a big bear down there on all fours in the dark and I don't know what that mail pouch looked like scooting across the ice ahead of me. So I got my voice way down in my throat and said to Charlie, 'What village is this?'

"I wish I could have seen Charlie's face. He just came out with the shakiest little voice and said, 'Sh-Sh-Shungnak!' But then I couldn't keep from laughing, and when Charlie knew who he was talking to he did another Santa Claus dance for me!"

Charlie took his ribbing gracefully and the party broke up. Marvin stuffed the school mail back into his pouch and we climbed the hill as light-hearted as two happy kids.

Before we started opening our precious letters from home, Marvin took time out to call the CAA station and report that he was back in Shungnak. "And you," he warned me, "had better learn how to use that radio!"

Three weeks later, when the river ice was ready for travel, Marvin and one of the village men went up by dog team to bring home our boat and motor still lying on the river bank. We didn't realize until then that the bottom of the boat was a mass of cuts made by sharp pieces of ice, some of them going halfway through the plywood floor.

"While your wife learn how to use that radio," Robert suggested after he had inspected the bottom of the boat, "maybe you better learn how you stay out of that river ice!"

CHAPTER XXIV

FINAL TRIP FOR JADE

We made our final trip up the Shungnak River late in the fall of 1947. The village began to feel concern about the possible commercialization of jade on a large scale and invasion into their own spot at the head of the Shungnak. There were other deposits along the Kobuk and up Dahl Creek, a tributary of the river near the village of Kobuk. The largest of the deposits was at Jade Mountain down below, some distance from Kiana; but at this point we all had an egotistic feeling that the Shungnak jade was superior in quality to any other in the Arctic and would be the most sought after.

"Nobody ever bother our jade before," argued Robert. "Maybe no need to worry."

"Things aren't like they were in your time, Robert," insisted one of the younger men. "I been to Fairbanks. I know. Sure thing some time anybody might come and take alla jade. Never can tell."

"He's right," Marvin defended him. "More and more

225

people coming to Alaska every day. They'll spread out and one day you'll see them this far north right into the villages. They'll know where the money is. You've got to protect your jade grounds and the only way to do it is to stake claims and work them."

So equipped with a supply of tin cans, pencil and paper, in addition to all the gear we had taken on our first trip, we started on a second. Uncle Ralph wasn't with us, but in his place we had Nelson Griest, Johnny Cleveland's son-in-law. Robert's son, Homer, joined our party too.

Marvin assumed we would make the trip in one day and arrive at Axel Knoll in time to camp for the night. But the rest of our team had a different idea. They hated to be hurried, and they loved to camp. So soon after we left the big river and started up the creek, they began to make remarks.

"This place would make a good camping spot."

"Maybe we better stop here."

Marvin heard all the remarks and knew what they meant, but he was at the helm running the motor and had no intention of stopping to overnight along the creek somewhere. Water was higher than we had ever seen it and we were travelling with a minimum of trouble, so he thought he had the situation under control. But as it turned out, he didn't.

Before long, little old Charlie Cleveland began to hold his hands over his stomach, wrinkle his face up in pain, and let out a soft moan once in a while. When he got no response, the pains got harder, the moans louder, and more frequent; and occasionally he would bend over, clutching his stomach, with his head almost down to his knees. Everyone but Marvin was showing great concern, and they finally cleared out a spot in the bottom of the boat for him to lie down. There was considerable Eskimo talk.

Then Robert said to Marvin, "We think the boat jiggling too much. It make Charlie sick."

Marvin squinted at his watch. "It's only another hour or so to Axel Knoll and Charlie will probably be all right in a little while."

226

But the moaning persisted, and finally Marvin slowed down the motor.

"Okay. You win. Where do you want to camp?"

They chose a spot a hundred yards below a nice sand bar and Marvin pulled up to the bank. Almost before the boat had stopped, Nelson jumped out with his machete in hand and started off into the brush swinging the machete from side to side, clearing a path as he went. Swarms of mosquitoes, disturbed from their resting spot in the deep grass and brush, rushed out at us. Marvin wasn't in a good mood to start with, and this didn't help. He hated mosquitoes.

Our companions hauled equipment out of the boat and into the woods on Nelson's path. Marvin and I thought they had all lost their minds. Here just above us was a nice clear sand bar and they were blazing a trail into mosquito-infested woods.

"What's wrong with camping on the bar?" Marvin asked.

He got a few odd glances and some polite mumbles, but no real reason from anyone as to why we should not use the bar.

"They're crazy!" Marvin commented as the last one trailed off with his bedroll into the brush. I agreed with him, and we motored on up to the bar to set up our own tent where the mosquitoes weren't so thick.

Our neighbors cleared out an area big enough to string up a couple of tarps for shelter, built a campfire, and began to boil up some young ducks they had shot on the way up the creek. We sat around to visit with them for a few minutes, then went back to our own tent and a cold supper, sprayed mosquito dope lavishly around, and crawled into our bags for the night. We were tired and the air smelled fresh, and we said how much fun it was to sleep outdoors. But for some reason, we couldn't get to sleep. The bar looked flat enough when we walked around on it, but lying down was something different. We kept rolling toward the water. A slope of just a few inches can make a lot of difference when you're trying to sleep. The sand was hard and riffled, and every ridge seemed to grind into us.

"Maybe we should have gathered some leaves or tall grass or something for padding under our bags," Marvin admitted.

"Yes, I suppose we should have. But I sure don't have the courage to get out in those mosquitoes again to do it, do you?"

"No! I'm already freezing to death and if we get out of these bags we'll get even colder and never will warm up."

"Say, Marvin," I recalled, "remember when we drove the tent stakes in, water began to seep into the stake holes just a few inches down? And it was ice cold too. We're right on top of it."

The dampness crept through the bags and our clothes into our skin. We shivered for hours; and as if all that wasn't bad enough, toward morning a cold brisk wind came up that almost ripped our tent from over us. We kept having to reach out and drive the stakes in a little deeper.

The sun came up early, but it was several hours before it had enough heat in it to do any good. We hadn't slept all night and ached from head to foot; so when the warmth finally penetrated the tent walls, we relaxed and warmed up enough to drop off to sleep, just in time for the Eskimo camp to start moving about and shouting back and forth to one another. We woke up to the sound of axes cutting firewood and the smell of coffee boiling and campfire smoke. It was time to get up and start our day's work.

Bleary-eyed and with splitting headaches, we crawled out, smoothed down our hair, washed in the creek, and sauntered over to the neighbor's camp with the cheeriest good mornings we could muster. We fought mosquitoes every step of the way through the brush until we reached their clearing with their smudge fires going and nary a mosquito in sight.

Nora was boiling mush. Everyone was washed and combed and well rested, just waiting for breakfast to be served while they swapped yarns and made boisterous jokes about nothing in particular.

Marvin vigorously rubbed his hands together. "That sun feels good. Sure got cold last night, didn't it?"

Everyone looked a little surprised.

"And then that wind this morning," he went on.

"I must be sleep," said Nelson. "I guess I never feel that wind."

When the whole crew shook their heads in bewilderment, Marvin decided to say no more. We just suffered in silence, grateful for the chance to warm our fingers over their fire and stay close to the smudge. We were happy to get on the river again where the sun could warm our frozen, stiff old bodies.

By mid-morning we had our camps set up at Axel Knoll and began the business of staking claims. The terrain was rough and the river did a lot of angling, so it was difficult to establish corners. But each one in the group finally selected a piece of land and drove stakes to mark the boundary lines.

Our next task was to write out the claim descriptions. Everyone had assumed that since Marvin was the teacher, he would be doing it; so they were a stunned crew when he insisted they would have to write their own.

"Nobody here know how to write that kind," protested Homer.

"Then there's no better time to learn than right now," declared Marvin.

With a sharp stick as a pencil, and the sand bar beside Axel Knoll for a blackboard, he drew pictures of claims with four corners and gave them their introduction to the language of land descriptions—the northwest corner of the southwest whatever it was, and so on and on. The only response he got was shaking heads and deep sighs.

"Well, I can see this isn't going to work trying to teach you all together," Marvin decided, "so we'll do it one at a time. Nelson, how about you first?"

Nelson unhappily struggled through this strange new vocabulary, repeating after Marvin a word at a time. But when he had to figure out a description by himself, he was at his wit's end. All the jibes and hilarity from the sidelines didn't help matters either.

"Wassa matter, Nelson? You forget that soon?"

"Maybe you too old to learn! Ya—ya!"

"Don't laugh at him," Marvin warned. "I'll bet nobody else can do any better. Teddy, you get up here and see if you can figure out what you're going to write on your paper for this corner right here." He indicated a corner of his sand map with the point of his stick.

One by one Marvin put everyone through his paces, with the laughing and teasing never ceasing; and the loudest laughs of all coming from old Johnny.

Johnny was one of the elders in the village, had a doting wife and family, and was definitely in the habit of being pampered and given special privileges. So when each of the other reluctant scholars had finished his mini course in staking claims, and Marvin said, "All right, Johnny, it's your turn now," the big grin froze on Johnny's face and his boisterous "ha ha" choked off right in the middle.

When the impact of Marvin's earthshaking statement became apparent to his already graduated students, the whole crowd broke into a storm of hilarity. They held their stomachs while they threw back their heads and yelled for sheer joy, danced up and down, and pointed their fingers at Johnny with a whole new round of "Yea, Johnny!"

The shoe was on the other foot, and Johnny was crushed. He protested like a little boy that he couldn't possibly learn anything; but his tormenters got behind him and pushed him into the center of the much-worked-over claim sketched out on the sand. Marvin began his routine all over again with a smile twitching at the corners of his mouth while he tried to act stern and teacherish. But when it came time for Johnny to repeat his northeasts and northwests, he simply said in a heartbroken little voice, "Putty hahd fo' ol' man."

So sympathy plus a little secret admiration for his showmanship overcame Marvin's severity, and Johnny was promptly excused from his class. Given an honorary degree without earning it, so to speak.

"Classes are finished now," Marvin announced. "Graduation's over. Everybody get busy and write out your claim descriptions!"

With considerable help from both Marvin and me, each one wrote out his four slips of paper. Then armed with four cans apiece and the papers, they made the rounds of their plots of land. The scraps of paper they folded up, placed one inside every can, and put a can upside down on top of each of the four corner posts. And the work was done.

* * *

Robert's son-in-law, Lawrence Gray, had his reindeer herd just a few miles across the tundra from us. So that afternoon Homer decided that instead of hunting jade, he would hike across country to visit Lawrence and his wife, Alice. He returned early the next morning with far more than just a visit to talk about. Lawrence had killed a black bear, so Homer came plodding into camp with a big chunk of fresh bear in his packsack.

Marvin and I had planned our menus a little better this trip than we had the first time we went jade hunting. We had brought along a small tin frying pan and a few powdered eggs. So when Homer offered us a piece of fresh bear meat, I told him I'd take a couple of steaks. Since native Alaskans boil ninety percent of their meat, it makes little difference to them how a carcass is cut up or what part each one gets. Homer's chunk of meat was just that— an irregular wiggly hunk with no definite shape.

"Don't know if I can cut off good steaks or not. Pretty hard when meat isn't frozen."

He did his best, but even then our meat was two inches thick in one spot and thin enough to see through in another. We didn't count bear among our favorite kinds of food, but after two days away from home and living in a tent eating cold snacks, anything would have tasted good. Marvin whipped up a brisk little camp fire, I laid a bloody looking piece of squishy dark colored bear meat into my frying pan, and squatted down beside the flame to fry it. With a handle six inches long and a pan made of thin

231

tin, two things happened. Not only did the outside of the steak burn black before the inside had warmed up, but my hand roasted right along with it. Even with the pan at arm's length, I felt my face burning too. So we settled for tough steak, raw in the middle, burned on the outside, and about as unappetizing as it's possible for anything to be.

"This stuff tastes terrible," I apologized.

"You can say that again! But I think it's the fault of the pan. You'd just about have to have a heavy iron skillet to do it right. Don't feel bad, though. We'll survive until we get home. Just don't try feeding me any bear meat again for a few years, though!"

While all this painful process was transpiring, we couldn't help but notice what was going on at the campsite a couple of rods away from us. The men had built their usual little camp stove from a ring of rocks supporting the top of an oil drum. While Nora heated a big kettle of hot water, Homer cut his bear meat into chunks of all shapes and sizes. They tossed the pieces into the pot and sat around the campfire squatting on their heels or propped up against trees, whittling sticks to pass the time, and carrying on their usual line of good natured bantering. When the meat was cooked, Nora ladled it into tin plates or bowls with an ample portion of broth over each piece of meat. Because spoons and forks were bothersome and not really needed for this particular meal, they picked the meat up in their fingers to chew off bite-size pieces; and when the meat was gone, they tipped the plates and bowls up to finish off the broth as though it were a cup of coffee. Nora sloshed off her dishes at the river bank, laid them out to dry, and the supper work was all done. The teachers had learned as much from the students as the students had learned from the teachers that day.

* * *

We had purposely delayed this trip until August in hopes of finding low water. By mid-summer the mountain tops were usually depleted of snow, so there were no tributaries pouring into the creek to swell its waters. And by the middle of August the summer rains had slowed, because Mother Nature was in the process of gathering her forces to convert balmy weather raindrops to early winter snowstorms. In that short interval between what had been and what was to be, the rivers were at their lowest levels. But this fall the dry season hadn't happened, so we finally conceded that we were running out of time and made the trip without further delay. The water made the trip up Shungnak Creek easier than our first one had been; but likewise it made it more difficult to wade the creek bottom in search of jade. So on our second day in camp, Marvin decided there were other things that needed doing.

"Ever since I first laid eyes on this gorge, I've believed that these rolling rocks and pebbles of jade we're finding didn't just happen. There's always a mother lode of gold somewhere, and I think there's got to be a concentrated source of jade somewhere too," was his theory.

"You think on other side this gorge we'll find big jade?" Charlie queried.

"That's what I think, Charlie. I'd like to walk through that gorge and see for myself. Anybody want to go with me?"

"Sure I go with you," Charlie offered.

Our two explorers took off on foot right after breakfast, packsacks on their backs, along the edge of the cliff above the gorge. Late that evening they came dragging back into camp. They had crossed the crest and looked at the creek on the other side—even crawled down to river level for a drink of water—but they were none the wiser as far as the source of jade was concerned. All they brought back to prove they had made the trip was a beautiful collection of color slides.

While Marvin and Charlie were Ponce de Leoning their way over the mountain, the rest of us spent our day in waist deep water in front of Axel Knoll looking, but finding very little jade. So on our third and last day, we changed our plan of attack.

"No use to stay here and look," Robert decided. "I think better some of us go up river and some go down river. Maybe we find better spots."

233

"Good idea," agreed Nelson. "If we can find more sand bar, then not so much water. Sand bar is best."

Most of the party scattered out, some going up river and some going down.

Marvin and Charlie, still exhausted from their tramp the day before, stayed close to camp as did Nora and I. Teddy Jack hunted close to camp, too. He was a strapping, healthy looking fellow in his late twenties; but he was an active tuberculosis victim and had hemhorraged several times, so was carefully restricting his activities.

While we five were alone in camp, Marvin waded out into midstream a few hundred feet downriver and discovered the biggest jade rock we had ever seen. It measured four or five feet across and about the same in depth.

He let out a big, "Hey! Come here! See what I found."

"What is it?" Teddy called back.

"You gotta come and see it. Come on!"

Teddy and I started down creek to see what he had found. Nora wasn't hunting that day and was busying herself with her housekeeping. Charlie was stretched out in his bedroll still recuperating, so it was left to the three of us to do something about our rock. Teddy managed to cross the current and reach the spot, but by the time I was in the river a few inches above my waist, I was losing my battle against the rush of the water. So I had to give up and keep my distance.

Marvin decided he and Teddy together could roll the rock to shore, but Teddy knew he should neither get his head under water nor exert the strength it would have taken. So they had to abandon that idea. The rock lay with its green side up, so we all agreed they should at least turn it over with the brown side exposed. This would make it less likely for anyone else to find it before we could get back up river with a crew of men to bring it out. So roll it over they did, and we marked the spot on the river bank to indicate where we should start looking for it on our return.

That time never came. Six weeks later Teddy bled to death from hemhorraging, and the following spring Marvin and I moved on to another village. Forty years have passed since I last saw Axel Knoll and the gorge and Shungnak Creek; and no one else is alive who knows where we left our marker.

CHAPTER XXV

BUSH PILOT

Archie Ferguson was the most amazing character in the whole Arctic. Everyone knew a little about him, and a few people knew a lot. But I'm sure no one ever knew everything about this short, plump, twinkly-eyed little guy with the raspy laugh and big grin. He was the most spectacular bush pilot that ever graced the Arctic, but actually he didn't do as much flying as many of the other pilots in the Kobuk country. It's just that he made a lot of history in a much shorter time.

Archie was a born extrovert with a big sense of humor. Whenever he carried a cheechako in his plane, he never missed the chance to cut out his motor unexpectedly somewhere along the way and then explain to his terrorized passenger that this always happened when you crossed the Arctic Circle. Once during the war years, when he called from the air for some high priority information, the voice at the control tower told him such information could be given out only in case of an extreme emergency. And Archie's reply, soon to become famous among his

237

Arctic neighbors was, "Any time I'm in the air, it's an emergency!"

Archie and his younger brother Warren were raised at their parents' gold claims on California Creek, somewhere up above Kobuk. They eventually moved to a spot between Shungnak and Kobuk where the elder Ferguson built a home for his family that was later sold to the federal government and became the CAA station. Archie learned to fly while the family was still living there.

"I had a helleva time learning how to set a plane down on that piece of muck up there," he told us once between cackly little laughs. "Every time my mother heard me coming, she'd stuff a stick of wood into the kitchen stove so I'd have some smoke coming out the chimney to give me some wind direction. I'll never forget the time she didn't have any wood on hand so she burned up my dad's best pair of wool trousers." Then the laughing stopped and he suddenly became thoughtful. "My dad never forgot it, either," he ended in a softer tone.

Our dealings with Archie weren't always the happiest ones, but for some reason he was one man you couldn't stay mad at forever. If he got the best of you in a bargain, he always did it with a smile on his face, and usually made up for it by doing you a favor of some sort in exchange. There was a lot of prestige in being able to spin a yarn to your peers on long winter evenings about the time you made a deal with Archie and came out on the short end.

But today I think back fondly on that fascinating little man and feel honored that I was fortunate enough to know him. There was a lot of good in Archie, and to hold your own in the Arctic you had to stand up and fight. He did.

Once a year when the government boat, the *North Star,* came up the coast from Seattle to Barrow, it stopped at major ports along the way to leave freight. Annual supplies for all the native villages in the Selawik, Kobuk, and Noatak valleys were unloaded at Kotzebue, then sent up the various rivers by barge. Archie, for years, had held the contract to lighter goods off the ship and deliver them to their final destinations. It was a thankless job and no way on earth could anyone have done it satisfactorily. There were constant repercussions and endless complaints from unhappy teachers when cases of food were broken into or fresh fruit was frozen solid on arrival. Regardless of where the real blame should be laid, it always landed on Archie's shoulders. He accepted it gracefully, and I doubt he ever lost a wink of sleep over it.

No way in the world could this busy little man personally supervise the lightering of cargo from ship to shore, storing it in his huge warehouse on the beach, then sorting and reloading it onto barges that made the journeys up the rivers. He had to hire local help for all his longshore work, and usually chose the most capable of the group to manage the operation. The warehouse was utter confusion and it was easy for a case of goodies to disappear behind a stack of lumber and never surface again.

We teachers soon learned that no way in the world could a case of mixed nuts or mushrooms or mandarin oranges escape all the pitfalls along the way. Such delicacies always left Seattle, but seldom lived long enough to see the end of the journey. Our wholesale houses cooperated as best they could with us on that score. Food most vulnerable to pilferage was packed inside other boxes labelled soap or sauerkraut.

The worst of the pilferage I think took place on the barges after they left Kotzebue. Archie supplied food and a cook for his men on the trips up river. But there were always unexpected delays; and when their own food supplies began runnng short, they made no secret of the fact that they helped themselves to whatever other stores they had on board that struck their fancy. Since a trip to the head of the Kobuk could take as much as two weeks, depending on high or low water, storms, delays in the villages or motor troubles, the Shungnak and Kobuk freight sometimes got hit rather hard.

There were other complications too. The barges never got underway until late August or early September. By this time the fingers of winter were creeping over the tundra, and rivers slowing up and lowering in depth in preparation for freeze-up. There was no way to protect the freight from freezing weather, so we seldom got our canned goods undamaged.

When you go for a year at a time without a taste of fresh bologna or wieners or a real potato or an egg with a shell on it, you can let yourself get carried away at the very thought of Archie's barge chugging around the bend. I remember the year we ordered the case of fresh celery. The barge arrived late in the afternoon when the sun had already set. Marvin was on the river bank to pick up our fresh goods as soon as it was unloaded. Whatever else came that night I don't recall; I only remember the fateful celery. Marvin pried open a board from the top of the box just to check it out. The poor thing had gone through so many freezings and thawings that it was a mess of mush. He could put his hand straight through it from top to bottom without touching much of anything solid.

He wiped his arm off the best he could on the frozen ground, hammered the box closed again with a stone; and leaving his cargo on the river bank he came storming up the hill in a fit of rage and disappointment.

"You should see that celery, Lou! Rotten! Rotten right to the bottom."

"Oh, no!" I wailed.

"Oh, yes! I'll just send that whole mess right back down to Archie and let him figure out what to do with it."

I agreed with him, but the more we thought about it, the more we wondered if possibly there might be a little bit of celery in the center of each bunch that was salvageable.

"We know very well that Archie won't do anything about it," I rationalized. "Even if he absorbed the price of the freight up river, we'll still have to pay for the celery plus all that freight from Seattle to Kotzebue."

Our annual supplies were ordered through the Alaska Native Service and they came up on a government boat from Seattle. The cost for goods and freight was taken out of our pay checks before we ever saw them, and our office was not inclined to listen to complaints.

The colder and darker and later it got, the more we wondered about our box sitting on the river bank. "If there *is* anything worth saving in that box, it won't last much longer. We aren't going to gain a thing by letting it sit there and freeze solid again. I suppose I could go down and get it."

So at ten o'clock Marvin pulled his parka off the top of the kitchen door where he always hung it, stuffed a flashlight into his pocket, and toted his celery up the hill. We spent the next two hours scooping the slimy outside layers off each bunch of celery down to the hearts that had somehow survived. We ended up with the equivalent of two or three bunches, but we nibbled it sparingly and paid our bill.

Archie's mail contract was a difficult one to fulfill. He was supposed to bring the mail up river once a month from June through September. The agreement was that he would carry it on his barge as he delivered freight, but it was apparent to everyone involved that the contract was an unrealistic one. He didn't haul freight once a month and it wasn't feasible to make the trip just for the mail. If we got two bargeloads of freight a week apart the last half of August, we also got two batches of mail. This qualified for two of the four months, but on the other two he sometimes had to default.

And of course everyone in the Arctic delighted in Archie's escapades as concerned the two catepillar tractors he had at the head of the Shungnak River.

We didn't realize when we made our visit to the Alaska-Kobuk Mining Company site near our jade deposits in 1946 that the tractors used in hauling some of the equipment in had never made it back to the river. There were two of them. They mired down somewhere along the trail where they sat for a good many years. It was Archie who finally decided the time had come to claim them a salvage and haul them out. How he got them across the tundra to the Kobuk, I'm not sure; but I believe he sent men in during the winter when the tundra was frozen, and that they warmed them up, started the engines, and drove them to the river bank on their own power. That proved to be the easiest and least spectacular part of the trip.

Archie had recently had built to his specifications a beautiful fifty thousand dollar tunnel barge with an inboard motor, and a a propeller inside the lower half of the structure. He used the boat first on his freighting up the Kobuk, and it made history all over the Arctic. Whole villages lined up on the river bank as it pulled in to shore just to see this remarkable contrivance and how well it operated. Archie gloried in his new toy. This may have been what brought on his hairbrained idea about salvaging the cats. The tractors were sitting on the river bank above Kiana waiting for a ride home, and Archie had instructed his crew on their last trip home at the end of the freighting season to load the cats onto the empty barge and take them in to Kotzebue.

The boys loaded the tractors like a crew of old pros and fastened them together with the biggest chain they had, but they failed to chain them to anything else. They parked them on the bed of the barge, equidistant from either side. Everything went fine until, just at the mouth of the Kobuk where the river enters Kobuk Lake, the water got a little rough. The barge began to list with the weight of water that had leaked into the bottom part; and with each listing, the cats slipped a little further to the low side. Finally it happened. The tractors skidded far enough to upend the barge; and still chained together, they flopped over into 20 feet of water.

It didn't take long for the news of the disaster to reach Kotzebue. Archie jumped into the closest airplane he could get his hands on and rushed to the mouth of the Kobuk. His crew that had intended to move on into port without their load, heard that plane from the time it left Kotzebue, and knew they'd better be doing something that looked at least businesslike before it reached them. So when Archie arrived, they had every available rope and chain dangling over the edge of the barge.

He zoomed in as low as he dared, opened his window, and circled on one wingtip around and around while he

242

yelled instructions to them as to how they should hook on to their lost tractors and haul them up again. Of course nothing happened, and a frustrated little pilot finally tootled off back to Kotzebue with his tractors in the bottom of the Kobuk.

There were always plenty of people standing by waiting to get a stab back at Archie for past grievances, and here was a chance. Someone reported him to the Coast Guard for obstructing a navigable river with dangerous machinery lodged at the bottom of the channel. Soon thereafter, he received a letter from the Coast Guard informing him that he was in violation and would have to remove his cats from the river.

Archie was ready for them. Every winter the villagers in Kotzebue, for lack of proper garbage facilities, stored all their trash, including honey bucket waste, in oil drums at the back doors of their cabins. Drums were plentiful in those days, since all the government installations used a fantastic amount of fuel every winter, and the drums weren't worth shipping back to Seattle. They were free for the taking. But come spring, something had to be done with the garbage. So just before breakup, barrels by the dozens were dog teamed out on the ice in Kotzebue Sound in front of the village, and left to disappear into the water when the ice went out.

Whether or not those drums at the bottom of the Sound ever interferred with Archie's lightering business is beside the point. The fact that they existed was enough. He sent a blistering message back to the Coast Guard that when the village of Kotzebue got rid of the hundreds of barrels that had accumulated in the ocean in front of the village over a period of years, he would get rid of his two tractors at the bottom of the Kobuk. So each side rested its case.

CHAPTER XXVI

LAST DAYS AT SHUNGNAK

The spring of 1948 was the logical time to make our first trip home. Cyndie, the oldest of our four children and our only daughter, was due in June; and we hadn't been able to make any suitable arrangements for her to be born in Alaska. That alone was a good reason for making a trip back to Wisconsin. But in addition to that, Marvin had made up his mind he would have to have a plane and learn to fly if we were to stay on in isolated villages with a baby in the house. That, too, called for a trip Outside.

We knew we would be coming back to Shungnak in the fall only long enough to ship out our personal belongings on the August barge and transfer to another village, so we began to spend an hour at the supper table every evening reminiscing on our three winters and two summers there on the Kobuk.

"Remember how naive I was about the whole thing when we first came?" I laughed one night. "I was afraid to go down to the village alone because I thought I wouldn't know how to talk to people."

"Well, I wasn't so smart myself," Marvin admitted. "I thought just because I'd been at Elim for a couple years that I knew all about the Eskimos, but I know now I didn't. I've learned as much here as you have about a lot of things—jade hunting, cabin building, boating, and how to deal with people—"

"I know. Sometimes I wonder if we haven't learned more from the people of Shungnak than they have from us."

"Oh, I wouldn't say that. We did a good job of teaching, and we did a lot of other things too. Getting that store built is the best thing that's ever happened to this village. Look at the size of the inventory we had last year as compared with our first year. I think it has more meaning for the village to know that we had to go it that first year alone before we could borrow our ten thousand. And George is doing well in the post office. They'll never be without a store or post office again, I'll bet."

"I think something will come of the jade eventually, too. Something where they make real money, I mean. I wouldn't be surprised to see the ANS step in and help them get some lapidary work going right here in the village."

"I still say something like that is the answer to a lot of village problems," Marvin added. "I don't think we've had as much bickering during the winter months since we have that store to keep people interested. Then of course the store and post office provide two families with an income; and if they could cut jade here, that would bring even more money into the village. That's what these villages need—craft work they can make right here and sell so they'll have some ready cash."

"Marvin, I'm going to miss Robert. And Irene, and the kids. I'm going to miss everybody, I'm afraid. I'll always remember how cute Mrs. Ticket looks when she comes up the hill to school every afternoon with all that willow and root under her arm!"

"You're right, Lou. I don't think we'll ever find another village we'll feel the same about. Shungnak is special."

Most of the village people had said good-by before they moved out to rat camp as soon as school was out. Each one, as he stopped by to have his last minute visit, thanked us for helping to establish the store and post office. It was evident that those two projects had made a lasting impression on them.

We had made arrangements with Bill Peterson weeks ahead of time to pick us up at Shungnak the first of April and fly us to Fairbanks so we could catch a plane on to Seattle or Minneapolis. This took considerable pre-planning on our part. We had to hold several Saturday sessions of school in order to complete our required number of days for the year. Since we had a coal furnace with a complicated hot water heating system, we had to have it all drained and the fire out long enough for the coals to cool before we left.

We systematically depleted our stock of perishable foods the last part of March, and packed our clothes we would need for the next four months. Early in the morning of April Fool's day, Marvin drained the hot water pipes, which meant we had no more heat. We had saved back only enough food for a cold breakfast, assuming that we would have lunch at a real restaurant in Fairbanks.

The house was cooling off rapidly. We had an extra amount of snow that winter, and most of it was still with us. By mid-morning we were shivering, so Marvin cut some kindling and started a fire in the kitchen range.

"We're safe with a wood fire," he said, "because this we can douse with a little water in a matter of minutes when Pete gets here."

We took turns every few minutes walking outside to listen for the sound of Pete's Stinson in the distance, but there was always total silence. By mid-afternoon we were too hungry to wait for the lunch in Fairbanks, so we opened up a can of beef stew and hurridly washed up the two cups and spoons we used. At eight o'clock we knew there wouldn't be any plane that day, so we opened our suitcase, dug out some nightwear, and went to bed early. We should have our sleep out by daylight, because surely Pete would be in the next morning as soon as he had light enough to fly.

A week later we were still building a small fire in the

kitchen range every morning, opening up a can of food at a time, washing two cups and two spoons in a big hurry after every meal, and going to bed early so we could be up with the sun.

All week long Marvin had worked with the transmitter, but we had hit one of those spells when radio waves seem to get lost in the doldrums, and there was nothing but static.

"I don't know why this had to happen right now," Marvin complained. "If I could just get out to Kotzebue I'd at least know what ails Pete and find out why he isn't getting in here. If he fools around much longer, the ice will be too rotten to land on."

The morning of the eighth day we suddenly heard the steady faint hum of a plane motor from down river.

"Airplane!" shouted Marvin, and we threw things together as fast as we could. Flip went beserk. He was everywhere at once, under our feet, on top of the luggage, jumping up at the windows, and letting forth with a continuous yap yap that deafened us both.

In a matter of minutes, the plane made a big circle of the village and lined up for a landing. Marvin started out the door to be on the river when it touched down, but he took one look at what was setting down at the end of the strip we had marked off with spruce boughs on the river, and stopped.

"That isn't Pete—it's Archie!" he called back to me.

For a few seconds he seemed deflated, then he brightened up again. "Maybe he'll take us in to Fairbanks. To heck with Pete!" And he disappeared over the crest of the hill.

I kept right on closing up suitcases and putting last minute things in order. Flip had gone down the hill with Marvin, so I was rid of him for a few minutes, at least. But then I heard the motor rev up and saw the plane taxi to the end of the strip for a takeoff, and I knew we weren't going with Archie. Minutes later Marvin and Flip were back.

"He can't take us," Marvin told me. "He has passengers

waiting for him in Kotzebue so has to go right back. But he says he'll tell Pete to get himself up here in short order. They've been socked in down there for a week and they're all behind schedule with their flying."

But when Pete didn't show up the next morning, we got desperate.

"I know what I'll do," I declared. "I'll start a project that can't be finished in two minutes like opening a can of beans. That should do the trick!"

So when Robert came up the hill for his daily conference with Marvin, I was in the midst of mixing up a batch of bread.

"What matter that Pete?" he asked. "I think I hear Archie say yesterday he tell Pete to come. If Pete come today, you don't bake bread!"

"That's why I'm baking the bread, Robert. Mark my word. Before this bread is finished, Pete will show up!"

Sure enough, that was all we needed. I had my sponge rising in the warming oven of the kitchen range when we heard that familiar hum of an airplane motor coming from down river. This time it was Pete.

"Good old Pete!" shouted Marvin. "I knew he'd come through. Best pilot in the Arctic!"

While Marvin and Flip made their dive down the hill, I began to clean up my mess of flour and shortening, mulling over in my mind who in the village had an oven so I could give away my sponge.

Then I heard the motor speeding up and the plane taxiing for takeoff. Oh, no! I thought, not another plane that isn't Pete!

Marvin appeared shortly, all smiles, and Flip an inch ahead of him all yaps.

"What's the matter this time?" I demanded, armed for battle.

"Nothing. It's too late in the day to start for Fairbanks and weather is deteriorating, so Pete says he'll be back in the morning. He'll go on to Kobuk tonight and stay with the Chaplains.

That was fine with us. We baked our bread and ate

a whole pan of hot rolls for supper. That night we retired early as usual, because now we really did have a reason for being up at daylight.

All three of us were on the river next morning when Pete's skiis slid to a halt. He jumped out to start loading in our gear as fast as possible, because time is always of the essence with a bush pilot in the Arctic. He's continually waging a battle against darkness and weather. But every last living soul in the village was at the plane too, and suddenly there was a whole round of handshakes and good bys that caused quite a delay. Pete, a big man to begin with, and looking twice as big in his sik-sik parka, showed his irritation. Then he suddenly wrinkled up his forehead and pulled his brows together as he asked me, "When are you going to have that baby?"

Embarrassed to no end, I said most meekly, "The last part of June. Why?"

Pete just shook his head and gave a big sigh. "That damn Archie," he grumbled. "He told me to get up here pronto because that kid was due any minute. And while I'm up here, he's probably stealin' the flying I had lined up to do in Kotzebue!"

Marvin was just in the process of hoisting the dog into the back seat. He turned his head and raised his eyebrows at me, as much as to say, "This isn't going to be the most pleasant trip in the world!"

Then I remembered. Pete was a bachelor. He lived in a one-room cabin in Kotzebue and cooked for himself except for the evenings he'd go over to the hospital and eat with Doc and the nurses.

"Look, Pete,! I said, "at what we're taking with us." I lifted the cover off my last pan of rolls I had tucked under my arm just enough so he could take a peek.

His eyes sparkled. "Home made bread!" he gasped. "Bless your heart, kid. Crawl into the back seat there with the pup!"

We settled into our seats, fastened our belts, and as I had done so many times in the past three years, watched the kids congregate behind the plane to get the blast of snow from the tail as Pete warmed up the motor. Then we made our turn and our takeoff with a mass of hands waving wild farewells from the river bank.

I leaned forward to shout into Marvin's ear above the roar of the motor, "Marvin, it just occurred to me—this will be the first time in almost three years that I've been more than twenty miles from Shungnak!"

As we circled to gain altitude before we nosed off to the southeast, I took one long last look at the spot that had been our honeymoon home. The big yellow school at the top of the hill suddenly seemed like a mansion to me. And the neat log building on the river bank with its proud sign, "Shungnak Coop Store, Post Office" implanted itself in my memory forever.

In a matter of seconds it seemed, the village diminished almost to nothingness. A stranger looking down from my seat might have called it a little black spot out in the middle of a mass of wasteland, just as I had mentally described it the first time I saw it from the air. But now it was no longer a little black spot of nothingness. Shungnak was a wonderful little world all of its own with friendly fires, cozy cabins, and warm-hearted people who taught the teachers, as together we built their small empire on ice.

EPILOGUE

During the eight years following our departure from Shungnak, Marvin and I moved on to three other villages: Unalakleet, Selawik, and Tetlin. Then came fifteen years on the Alaska Highway operating a roadhouse and our own air taxi service. There we raised our four children. Twenty nine years after we left our first village, one of my sons flew a party of people on a five-day trip across the Arctic, and I went with them. We spent our first night at Shungnak.

I hardly recognized my village. The federal government had moved all but two or three of the families from the river bank to the top of the hill beside the school. They lived in three-bedroom houses built of lumber brought in from the lower states. They had central heating, a power plant that provided electricity, telephones, daily air mail service, and satelite T.V.

Our school had just been torn down and replaced by a new, modern building and a huge gym; with a staff of teachers and aides to provide an enriched education to the sons and daughters of those parents who had been our students back in the 1940's.

Yes, our school kids had grown up, stayed on in their village, and married one another. But in 29 years, they hadn't forgotten. We were given a royal welcome such as I had never seen before. And that night we all sat in a circle on the floor of the gym while the photography teacher set up his projector, and we spent two hours looking at color slides I had saved those 29 years and brought along with me. The walls of the huge room surrounding us seemed strange and out of place to me, but the faces in the circle around me were as familiar as though I had never been away. We laughed together at the antics of the children of the 1940's, and were hushed and sober at the pictures of those who were no longer there.

I went to sleep that night with a great peace of mind, realizing that although they had changed the physical face of the village, they could never change the hearts of the people.

* * *

A tragic plane crash at Shungnak just prior to my visit had taken the lives of several of the local residents, including the young man who had so gloriously danced his Santa Claus suit away at our Christmas program. And well over 30 years after we left the village, a man who had been one of our students found the propeller blade we lost the day of our fateful boat wreck in 1946.

254